MAYA
COLOR
THE PAINTED VILLAGES OF MESOAMERICA

◆ ◆ ◆ ◆ ◆

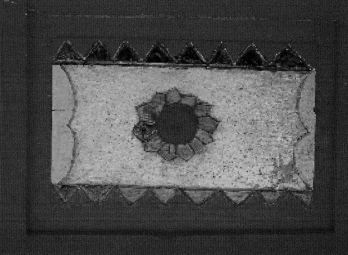

PHOTOGRAPHS BY JEFFREY BECOM
TEXT BY JEFFREY BECOM AND SALLY JEAN ABERG

MAYA COLOR

THE PAINTED VILLAGES OF MESOAMERICA

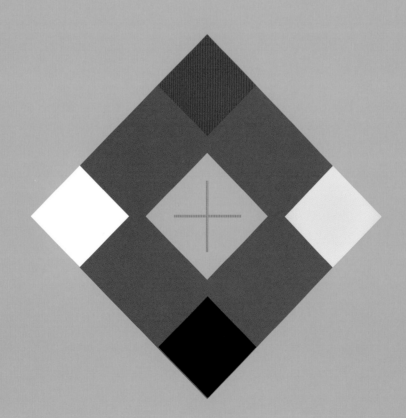

ABBEVILLE PRESS PUBLISHERS
NEW YORK ◆ LONDON ◆ PARIS

JACKET FRONT: *Rainy Season, Xela, Quezaltenango, Guatemala*
JACKET BACK: *Two Musicians, Bonampak, Chiapas, Mexico*
ENDPAPERS: *Rosalila Red, Copán, Honduras*
HALF TITLE: *Door with Flower, Santa Eulalia, Huehuetenango, Guatemala*
FRONTISPIECE: *Turquoise Lintel, San Juan Ostuncalco, Quezaltenango, Guatemala*
RIGHT: *Primary Wall, Cosamaloapan, Veracruz, Mexico*
CONTENTS: *Pink Chevron, Flores, El Petén, Guatemala*

EDITOR: Jacqueline Decter
DESIGNER: Nai Y. Chang
PRODUCTION EDITOR: Abigail Asher
PRODUCTION MANAGER: Lou Bilka
MAP: Sophie Kittredge

First edition
2 4 6 8 10 9 7 5 3 1

Library of Congress Cataloging-in-Publication Data
Becom, Jeffrey.
Maya color : the painted villages of Mesoamerica / photographs by Jeffrey Becom ; text by Jeffrey Becom and Sally Jean Aberg.
p.   cm.
Includes bibliographical references and index.
ISBN 0-7892-0215-8
1. Mayas—Dwellings.   2. Maya painting.   3. Church buildings—Central America.   4. Church buildings—Mexico.   5. Symbolism of colors—Central America.   6. Symbolism of colors—Mexico.   I. Aberg, Sally Jean.   II. Title.
F1435.3.D84B43   1997
701'.85'089974152—dc21   97-8347

CONTENTS

Two Pomegranates
Antigua Guatemala, Sacatepéquez, Guatemala

OPPOSITE
Calla and Cross
Villa las Rosas, Chiapas, Mexico

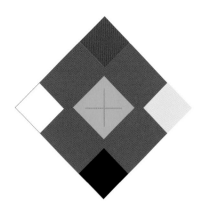

INTRODUCTION
THROUGH THE DOOR OF COLOR

Color—and the symbolic ways that the Maya of Mexico and Central America use painted color on their homes, places of worship, and dwellings for their dead—has been my obsession for the past eight years. What began with simple curiosity—Why are so many Maya tombs painted jade green?—evolved into a long and intricate journey undertaken with my wife, Sally. Together we explored ancient Maya color traditions and their fruit, the painted villages of today's living Maya.

As we scratched beneath the surface of their paint, Maya voices carried us forward in our search. "My house is blue, the color of water and the heavens. Without these the world would

end," said Eliseo Uk as he gathered herbs near the Uxmal ruins in the state of Yucatán, Mexico. Ten-year-old Angel, of San Andrés Xecul, Guatemala, proudly declared, "Many visit our yellow church. They leave contented." And while weeding around her mother's turquoise headstone in the La Palma, El Salvador, cemetery, Doña Candelaria explained, "We paint to honor the souls of our ancestors. One day my children will shelter my soul with color."

I come to *Maya Color* as a photographer and painter with formal training as an architect. These three pursuits inspire one passion: painted walls. As a boy growing up in rural Indiana, I remember painting local scenes in oil on canvas and wondering why my neighbors' barns were nearly always red. Investigating this color custom, I learned that frugal farmers simply chose the least expensive pigment around— red rust—to best hide barnyard grime. To this day I remain fascinated by what colors a building wears and why. For the past two decades I have immersed myself in the study of painted traditional architecture and how its cloaks of color are embraced, altered, or abandoned over time.

Mam House, San Martín Sacatepéquez, Guatemala

Painted façades offer me subject and palette from which to derive my own artwork as I, in turn, document their brilliance and power.

The first walls I focused on were the grand stone monuments of Europe, but my small-town beginnings and painter's tempering soon drew me to the more humble but colorful homes of farmers and fishermen in the lands bordering the Mediterranean Sea. Seeking the meanings behind their marvelous colors, I asked Moroccan housewives why they shield their entryways in cerulean blue. I questioned an Italian shrimper about his town's unique green doors and gleaned the recipe for this pistachio tint. Puzzling over the reason nearly all Greek houses are whitewashed, I discovered the isolated eastern islands, where villages compete with one another in bold hues. Along the way I found that Mediterranean color can disguise poverty, dissuade insects, argue politics, and deflect the evil eye. Paint also provides a small opportunity for creativity and control in a world otherwise ruled by church and nature, at the same time that it echoes the color symbolism of classical Greece and Rome.

Color thus declared itself my life's calling, whether I captured color histories, myths, and meanings with camera, brush, or words. Twelve years of travel and inquiry overseas led to the publication of my first book of photographs, *Mediterranean Color,* and a PBS documentary, *For the Colors,* that followed me as I photographed my way across Italy. It was during the making of this film that I truly felt the twentieth century nipping at my heels as it laid claim to even the most secluded hill towns and their painted colors. Surrendering the field, I turned my gaze in a new direction. From long familiarity with Old World ways, it was now only natural for me to venture into the "New World" that was first unmasked and then transformed by my old friends, the Mediterraneans. And so I journeyed south of my own country's border. Mexico's colors were magnetic. I was pulled southeastward, farther from the tourist trail and further back in time, until I reached Veracruz State, a region rich in traditional cultures and the gateway to the Maya world. With their ties to a painted past so tantalizing, the Maya summoned. My path was set.

The Maya had already captivated Sally. Years before I moved to San Francisco, where we first met, her aunt had bequeathed an intriguing diary of a rugged trek through Guatemala in the 1940s. Fortunately for me, Sally also loves to travel and is gifted with two handy skills I lack: an extraordinary memory and a sense of direction. A native Californian,

Rural Devotion
Santiago Atitlán,
Sololá, Guatemala

Calle Noche Triste
Oaxaca, Mexico

Embroidery for the Soul
Pomuch, Campeche, Mexico

she holds a degree in English and another in art history that was prompted by an enchantment with the dazzling palette of fauvist painters. She earned her living as a journalist and researcher before working for more than a decade with the renowned Pacific Film Archive of Berkeley's University Art Museum. Sparked by the same expressive colors that were fast becoming my preoccupation, Sally needed no persuading to join me on many of my Mediterranean tours and only a little coaxing to stretch her sense of adventure and tackle the new Maya terrain. In addition to her contributions as journal-keeper, navigator, occasional translator, and editor of both my writing and images, Sally now steps forward as coauthor of this book. For simplicity's sake, however, we have chosen to tell our story in my first-person voice.

To define the project, Sally and I smoothed open a new map and flagged our territory: the ancestral world of the Maya. It lies cradled within Mesoamerica, the great arc of land that sweeps from central Mexico down through Panama's spindly tail and has nurtured five thousand years of civilizations. Today the Maya homelands encompass six states of southern Mexico—Chiapas, Yucatán, Campeche, Quintana Roo, Tabasco, and Veracruz—plus Guatemala and portions of Belize, Honduras, and El Salvador. All told, this area is just half the size of Texas and only fifteen hundred miles around; but ancient Maya trade routes often swept us beyond these bounds to places and peoples heir to Maya painting and belief. With this straying and all our zigzagging and backtracking, we logged more than 100,000 miles on our Maya color quest.

En route we collected stories of the paint while my camera claimed the patina on a corn yellow shutter lashed against a blood red wall, smoke-blackened *santos* shouldering countless petitions in their sky blue chapel, and the shadowed niche of a jade green tomb. As Sally and I absorbed these images and words, we began to grasp that, to the Maya, what is painted is important. Color engenders life. It is creation and a magical medium of faith. These revelations, in turn, established our themes: the painted places of shelter, devotion, and burial.

Following the Maya from house to church to grave,

we traced the lineage of changes wrought on Mesoamerica since the conquistadors first cut a wide swath through indigenous cultures. The Spanish Conquest decimated millions and unleashed the greatest migration of all time, building an empire on native lands and backs. Despite the enormity of this assault, we gradually recognized that the Old World does not have as firm a grip on the New World as first appears. Especially here among the Maya, Mediterranean beliefs are often merely grafted onto resistant native stock. Five centuries' efforts to crush vernacular traditions have only plowed these just beneath the surface, for the chronicle of the Maya did not begin with Columbus or Cortés but speaks of kings and customs rooted millennia before Christ and Catholic monarchs were planted in this soil.

Many studies treat the Maya as one of history's curious, closed chapters; but this ancient culture is far from extinguished. Today over seven million Maya populate their ancestral realm. Speaking some thirty distinct Mayan tongues and often only a few words of Spanish, these Maya are classified by their language group but call themselves by their village name. They hail from thousands of hamlets scattered across frosty mountains, scorching deserts, and steaming jungles. Their cherished landscape, littered with the ruined cities of glorious ancestors, must now be shared with mestizos (people of mixed blood) and a powerful elite of pure Spanish descendants. The state and national borders that these "newcomers" have drawn across the age-old domain mean little to the Maya, who view their own village as the center of the world. But with these imposed boundaries, the intruders lay claim to hallowed Maya land—the very cornerstone of traditional life—and thus consign the modern-day Maya to the least of everything: food, wages, education, justice, opportunity, years of life, and fertile soil. Yet the Maya endure. Treading a path beaten hard by century upon century of repetition, they continue to sow their deified corn, commune with their gods, and paint life into their color-washed village walls. For Sally and me it is this painted color that most loudly broadcasts the message of Maya survival.

Long ago, every Maya citizen could read the cycle of

Maize
Zunil, Quezaltenango,
Guatemala

his life, his land, and all creation in five symbolic pigments: the red of blood, birth, and beginnings; the yellow of sustaining corn; the blue-green of crucial water and fertility; the black of death; and the white of change. To make sense of their world, the ancient Maya created a sacred map binding the four cardinal directions and center to these five vital colors. The red of the east's essential sunrise blazed from its apex. The Maya then assigned everything in their universe to the colors in this diamond. Gods, corn, winds, birds, bees, trees, epochs, planets, and plagues were each allied with a compass point and its hue. This cosmic map once oriented Maya architecture, and its emblem was abundant in carving and design. Today the map lives on within the diamond patterns so prevalent in Maya weaving, pottery, and even village plans. We can also read its latent meanings in painted color glowing all across the Maya world, from vivid houses in the cloud-bound Guatemalan highlands to resplendent churches in waterlogged Tabasco State to the parched Yucatán Peninsula, where deep-dyed cemeteries bloom with brush strokes.

Once Sally and I fathomed the resonant power of these colors, we firmly fixed the diamond map as *Maya Color*'s graphic setting. We tied its five symbolic hues to our five paint-drenched chapters: the red of beginnings for the dawn of Maya colors, the yellow of harvest and hearth for painted houses, the blue-green of divinity for painted churches at the heart of our text, the black of death for painted cemeteries, and the white of change for chromatic shifts within today's Maya realm. This is not to imply that a color bears only one message for all Maya, nor that every house is yellow or every tomb is black. Even neighboring villages may have separate color customs, and both yellow and white have lost much clarity of meaning over the centuries. Other inconsistencies arise because the living Maya run the gamut from culturally isolated and ritual bound to integrated and progressive. But like a child's string telephone—with one tin can resting on a pyramid and the other in the hands of a modern heir—color serves

as the connective cord. Knowledge of the ancient diamond map stretches this line taut; and through paint's pregnant whispers, we detect a remarkable continuity reverberating across time.

Enthusiastic travelers have been recording the Maya world ever since the camera's nineteenth-century birth coincided with the first excavations of ancient sites. Sally and I follow in the footsteps of these devotees. This book presents our personal view of the Maya through the door of color swung open by two decades of educating our eyes. Ours is not a mysterious expedition into uncharted territory, nor do we approach with extraordinary equipment or years of academic training in this field. But our lack of specialized degrees has not necessarily been a hindrance. For 150 years Maya scholars have wrangled over far-flung theories fluctuating as rapidly as the Mexican peso. Since we began our study with few preconceived ideas, we bravely—or perhaps foolishly—felt free to join the fray with some hypotheses of our own.

Attempting to confirm these hunches, we dispatched ourselves on a series of circuitous routes, open to any plausible, if possibly apocryphal, stories to come our way. Gradually, color conjectures from daily observations and conversations in the field, when assisted by inductive leaps and substantiated by intensive research, produced our most persuasive color insights. The Maya were revealed to us through a great many written sources: translations of those few pre-Hispanic bark paper codices that survived jungle rot and Spanish clerics' flames; both native and conquerors' eyewitness accounts of the conquest; colonial-era histories; explorers' tales and the romanticized notions of eccentrics; dusty anthropological tomes and dissertations; contemporary travel writers; and updates from today's Mayanists, who continually add new pieces to the gigantic jigsaw puzzle of this labyrinthine culture.

Each time Sally and I crossed our southern border, we rejoiced as orderly blocks of mirrored glass and gray concrete gave way to unruly purples, pinks, and aquas. Our life

EAST

NORTH

SOUTH

WEST

on the road in two- to nine-month stints was travel at its most basic. Making decisions from hour to hour, we followed weather, festivals, and color legends rather than a fixed itinerary. There was no such thing as a wrong turn, since every Maya hamlet held painted promise. We prospected between bases in our little Honda Civic or any conveyance at hand, from rented jeeps, donkey carts, and dugout canoes to three-wheeled bicycle taxis, frigid luxury buses, and rides atop beets or carrots in the back of pickup trucks. Mostly, however, we bounced along in thirdhand, jam-packed, brightly painted Blue Bird buses, possibly the very same ones we rode in to grade school, though our seat mates here were often live chickens and goats. But no matter our means of transport, upon arrival we always slowly combed each street on foot, paid homage to the church, and sought out the cemetery with the pace, perspective, and priorities of a villager.

Because we walked up to twelve hours a day, I limited myself to the weight of one trusty Nikon F3 and a 35mm Nikkor perspective-control lens. My Kodak Lumiere film and batteries had to endure grueling extremes of heat and humidity, but risk of losing exposed film to border theft, military confiscation, or unreliable shipment home was of even greater concern. I will never forget the concise but devastating tracking report, *"El camino es frío"* (The trail is cold), from an international carrier that misplaced two months' worth of my work for several weeks before fortuitously recovering the package.

Getting in sync with life in the land of the Maya entailed far more than simply resetting watches. On many occasions Sally and I shared hotel rooms with lizards, scorpions, bats, bees, and the most insecticide-proof cockroaches in the world. We politely sampled—or even more politely declined—such local delicacies as wriggling red worms, insect eggs, armadillo tacos, grilled jungle rodents, and roasted winged ants sprinkled with salt and lime. We found ourselves complimenting exotic home decor like snakeskins, monkey skulls, and stuffed foxes as if these were as common as concrete geese on an Indiana porch. We often just missed hurricanes, narrowly avoided prowling pumas, and talked our way out of thousands of dollars in bogus *infracciónes*. We

were sometimes laid low by poisonous jungle thorns and by innocent-looking *ensaladas* harboring intestinal attack. And we were frequently stalled by guerrillas' felled trees, government roadblocks, army maneuvers, and cross-examinations by crisply pressed, no-nonsense officers searching for drugs in the middle of nowhere.

From Acancéh to Zacalaca and a host of villages in between, we spoke with a curious cast of characters: embassy consuls and election observers; birders and B-girls; *beisbol* stars and Bible-thumpers; Mennonites and Mormon teens on missions; poets and expatriates; archaeologists and hippies; weathered mercenaries wound too tight and tourists on vacation; as well as volunteers from the Peace Corps, Habitat for Humanity, and Amnesty International. We met a missionary who said she'd known Maya children to die for lack of a thirty-cent pill, and a coffee baron's wife ensconced in a posh fortress who longed for the old days of strong dictators when both she and her possessions were safer. We encountered a pair of retired American optometrists who were heartbroken over a nearly blind Maya woman—carried on her hopeful grandson's back the twenty hard miles to their door—because they could do nothing but fit her with a pair of sunglasses. And then there was the Miami restaurateur living in Belize who bragged about all the jade he'd looted from Maya sites and smuggled back to the States in his wife's brassiere.

But mostly we talked with the Maya themselves: farmers, brick makers, waiters, mothers, mechanics, grave diggers, barbers, potters, paint-shop clerks, and shamans—all keepers of the colors of their world. Some dwell in the richest bastions of traditional culture and color, like the cool mountains of Chiapas and Guatemala or the flat, searing Yucatán. Others persevere in Belize or El Salvador, where Maya colors, languages, costumes, and memories have nearly faded away. The rest live in between, in the growing tangent where pure Maya meet change. All have a story to tell about color. "The Days of the Dead are over. Tonight we dance the spirits back to their painted homes," explained the woman loaded down with calla lilies, following the setting sun to her colorful village cemetery. "I paint my house

Ladder and Bull
Coacoatzintla,
Veracruz, Mexico

16

Green Chair with Hibiscus
El Abrevadero,
Veracruz, Mexico

with red and yellow so I can see it from my field across the valley," said the Maya melon farmer, leaning on his hoe. And in a colorless refugee camp in southern Mexico, where no money for food meant no money for paint, we listened to a Guatemalan who had fled the civil war with nothing but his hunger. He yearned for his distant cornfield, his patron saint, and the guidance of his ancestors. "I will only live again," he sighed, "when I see my village and our blue church. If one day I can go home."

By now there are some half-dozen Maya families we visit on every trip. "It's a miracle; you have returned!" they exclaim. First we catch up on marriages and babies, the status of their corn, the shiny antenna that may have sprouted from the thatch roof, and of course the coats of colors, fresh or fading, on their village walls. Then, around a meal of beans and tortillas, we share photographs from our journeys. Our hosts ask voraciously, "Where is this, and this?" of places that are far outside their narrow sphere even if just a few miles away. Sometimes they puzzle over our fascination with houses we neither built nor live in, altars

Girl with Hen, San Antonio Palopó, Guatemala

we do not worship before, and tombs our people will never occupy; but they always appreciate our record of their polychrome village. They know these images mark the path that each will one day take in slow procession from beloved house, past precious church, into a painted grave.

Before leaving any of these friends, we offer to take family snapshots. Children are collected, and everyone lines up outside. A teenage daughter, who has changed into festival best, runs to catch her prized red hen for the shot. A dignified grandfather repositions his sombrero and then stands frozen at attention beside his wife. While Sally teases out a few smiles, I shield stray sunbeams with my straw hat

and release the shutter. On our next visit we deliver the prints and watch as work-toughened hands tenderly wrap the paper treasures with brilliant woven cloth to store them safely inside a painted wooden trunk or flat upon their altar like some priceless relic.

Maya Color does not profess to be a comprehensive survey of the Maya. Both images and text revolve solely around color. In our series of vignettes, dialogues are telescoped, eliminating most of the preliminaries about family, corn, and ancestors as well as the third party sometimes assisting with translation, since we speak little Mayan. Thus conversations are unmanipulated but distilled. The same is true of the images; for while my photographs are documentary, I do control and transform by limiting what, when, and how I shoot. I avoid everything that would distract from my true commitment—painted color—including traditional landscapes and portraits. This may be just as well. Maya feel invaded by tourists who snap away without permission or recompense, and fear persists that a photograph in the wrong hands can be used to work evil against the person pictured. Such concern is well-founded in politically volatile areas, where photographs that identify can also mark to kill.

To further emphasize color, I shun direct sunlight's patterning shadows. I also censor suffering, soda bottles, and electric lines from my frame, composing an idealized world of timeless refuge. Maya culture is thus more complex and contradictory than my photographs suggest, and certainly less idyllic, but it is no less colorful. Anyone who has wandered through a Maya village will agree that my images are there, intact, awaiting patient discovery: offerings of first fruits resting on a yellow church ledge; the skull reverently placed atop a green tomb; the crooked ladder balanced against a deep red wall; or hibiscus flowers fallen to fade beside a green chair upon a blue-dyed porch.

In our pursuit of color, Sally and I spend much time making contact and earning trust, grateful for any color clues. At every opportunity we ask, "What do the colors mean? Are they important? Have you heard stories about why this is painted?" If these questions lead nowhere, we try to enter through a backdoor, asking, "When do you paint? How is the paint made? What colors will you choose?" Sally's extensive note taking intrigues the Maya even more than my camera, because her journals manifest something beyond the sound of a click. Time and time again our endlessly repeated interview nets the evasive or honest but unfulfilling answer, "It is the custom." With this, our kind Maya informants loudly proclaim cultural continuity. But these words do not establish proof of the color diamond's tenacity, even when we see it evidenced in their paint. Many factors conspire against communication: multiple language barriers, lost keys to the color code, and most of all the impenetrable veil of secrecy surrounding all that is considered sacred.

It is difficult to draw a portrait from a shadow, but this challenge only makes the rare discovery more satisfying. Whenever we fear that we are off track in our theories, a Maya will invariably steer us back on course. "Why is your church altar painted red?" we inquire of a Maya elder. "To please San Miguel. He brings the rains to our soil," he replies. "But why red?" I pursue. "Because we like the color." "And for any other reason?" "It is our custom." "I have heard that your ancestors often painted their great temples red," I prompt. "Well, of course," he confirms with evident excitement. "Red is the color of the blood of Jesus and of the sunrise, which we need to live." A covert belief has been confided, and we have our reward, that ancient link: the red of East and precious blood. The red of beginnings.

Painter's Hands, Hoctun, Yucatán, Mexico

GULF OF MEXICO

Mexico City ⋆

● Tlaxcala

🏛 **CACAXTLA**

Puebla ●

Xalapa ●

Veracruz ●

VERACRUZ

Tlacotalpan ●

MARITIME TRADE ROUTE OF THE PUTUN MAYA

🏛 **COMALCALC**

San Isidro
Guaytalpa

TABASCO

Villahermo

PALEN

M
E
X
I
C
O

Oaxaca ●

Bochil ◆
Larrainzar ◆
Chamula ◆
San C
de

Tuxtla
Gutiérrez ●

Zinacantan ◆

PAN AMERICAN HIGHWAY

CHIAPAS

PACIFIC OCEAN

San Antonio Sac

San Ju
San Martín
Quezaltena

🏛 **ANCIENT CITY**
⋆ country capital
◇ state capital
◆ city
✦ village

0   50   100   150 MILES

0   50   100   150 KM

Río Lagartos

YUCATÁN

• Mérida
Hoctun
Kantunil
CHICHÉN ITZÁ
Valladolid

Isla Mujeres

Cancún

ATLANTIC OCEAN

MAYAPAN
Muna   Tekit

Nunkini
Calkini

Isla Cozumel

JAINA

UXMAL

TULUM

Dzitbalché
Pomuch

• Campeche

Felipe Carrillo Puerto

N

San Andrés Noh-Ca

QUINTANA ROO

CAMPECHE

CARIBBEAN SEA

Chetumal

BELIZE

El Petén

Belize City

Lake Petén Itzá   **TIKAL**

Flores   **TAYASAL**

Najá
YAXCHILÁN

Belmopan

Lacanjá

ONAMPAK

acandon Jungle

CARACOL

Bay Islands

FOURTH VOYAGE OF COLUMBUS

San Mateo Ixtatán

Todos Santos
Cuchumatán
Aguacatán
Huehuetenango

Trujillo
Tela   La Ceiba
Ilamapa

GUATEMALA

stenango
San Pedro Jocopilas
San Sebastián Lemoa
Chichicastenango

COPÁN

HONDURAS

ecul

Sololá
KAMINALJUYÚ
Antigua   Guatemala City
Lake Atitlán

Gracias
La Campa
Caiquin

La Palma

Tegucigalpa

**JOYA
DE CERÉN**

Izalco   **EL SALVADOR**

NICARAGUA

San Salvador

CHAC

1
BEGINNINGS
THE DAWN OF COLOR

Outscaled and overwhelmed, Sally and I have lost all sense of what we're stepping into. In this verdant purgatory of eternal twilight known as the Lacandon Jungle, everything is oozing, spongy, festering, and wet. Pilgrims of color, we are trekking toward the richly frescoed Maya temple at the twelve-centuries-old ruins of Bonampak. This day will fulfill a long-anticipated mission to venerate and photograph the treasured colors on its walls. Since Bonampak harbors the only complete set of ancient Maya murals in existence, we willingly submit to this punishing limbo. Fierce thorns tear through our clothing. Mud sucks at our inadequate shoes, mocking us with a rhythmic squish. Sweat streams down our faces, carrying with it bug repellent,

Procession of the Musicians
Bonampak, Chiapas, Mexico

OPPOSITE
Stone Portrait
Palenque, Chiapas, Mexico

which burns our eyes yet is clearly no deterrent to legions of feasting insects. Less than a mile out, we are already caked in muck up to our thighs. Trudging upon a dark humus that fuels ever-new shades of green, we grapple our way past mutant houseplants and clamber around the flaring roots of titanic cedars, ceibas, and mahoganies whose branches labor under their load of ferns. All around us, twisting lianas braid their way into the heavens some fifteen entangled stories overhead. On we navigate through an emerald sea without leaving a ripple. The rain forest simply closes about us as we pass.

Slowly our eyes adjust to the green gloom, and chlorophyll's monochrome gives way to full spectrum. High overhead a Technicolor parrot, startled, shrieks and pierces the canopy, dropping a ripe red cashew fruit to explode at our feet in the velvety yellow moss. Pincushions of phosphorescent mushrooms glow a toxic crimson from the forest floor. Gigantic butterflies, blue as gas flames, dip and glide like kaleidoscopic jewels, floating upward until swallowed in thick shadow. Turquoise hummingbirds with ruby breasts fire past our heads like prismatic bullets among leaves the size of parasols. For years Sally and I have sought the origins of Maya color in painted village walls. But only now, sloshing down this tortuous trail as colors glitter, flash, and detonate around us, do we finally recognize their primeval source.

Blue and Gold Macaw

Steaming on the lowland border of Mexico's southeasternmost state of Chiapas, the Lacandon Jungle forms the sheared western edge of the last great rain forest left on our continent. When this jungle jumps the frontier into Guatemala, it is called El Petén. It does not end until it laps the slopes of the Maya Mountains of Belize. Over a thousand years ago this pulsing green heartland of Classic-era culture propelled sixteen million Maya to splendorous heights, a fact that strains credibility as our own advance is strangled by a squeeze of sticky creepers and organic barbed wire. Stumbling, we grab dangling vines that coil like venomous snakes; by now, everything menaces. Fear cooks up a rich bacterial stew spiced with burrowing botfly larvae, bloodsucking leeches, disfiguring rashes, and fatal infections with long, terrifying names.

This is hardly the Sunday stroll we had been promised; but then Bonampak, one of a galaxy of ancient cities cocooned in this forest, has never been easy to reach. Just yesterday in Palenque—a flea-bitten dog of a town as grubby as its namesake ruins are glorious—we had scoured for options to reach the site and found them limited to one. The tinny four-seater plane that occasionally sputters in was grounded by the jungle-based Zapatista revolution that had put all Mexico on edge, alert, and notice with its call for land and justice. So we were left with the man who knows a man who has a van who can take us to a village where there's a guide who knows the way. *"No problema, no problema,"* he reassured, thumbing our pesos over and over as we grilled him on the status of the cease-fire and route. No expedition clothing or equipment needed, and we'd be back in time for supper. I suppose we wanted to be convinced.

Shivering in the damp air well before dawn this morning, we waited expectantly on the appointed street corner. Eventually, a ravaged VW van choked up to the curb and expired at our feet. Suppressing our concerns, we piled in. After a few false starts of the spent motor, a triumphant smile crossed the face of Carlos, the driver, and we three chugged off through the garbage-strewn town. By the dim glow of dash lights, Sally and I surveyed the interior. What wasn't gnawed, stabbed, cracked, or burned was smeared, patched, or wired together. Veterans of cheap hotel mattresses, we huddled at one end of a listing seat, contorting to avoid the protruding springs and moldy stuffing. The windows were too grimy for view, and the windshield sported a spiderweb of fractures. But no matter; we could measure our progress through gaps in the rusted-out floor. Carlos, evidently intimate with this empty stretch of road, soon took to driving on either shoulder rather than resort to the highway itself, which was more pothole than pavement.

Three times we were halted at spiked barricades where government soldiers' wary eyes peered from behind camouflaged sandbags festooned in razor wire. And three times these bleary-eyed, uniformed adolescents with acne and automatic weapons painstakingly inspected our passports by flashlight and then politely frisked me and the pitiful van for *pistolas*. *"¿Periodistas?"* (Journalists?) they interrogated with as much authority as youth could muster. "Tourists for the ruins" always won our release.

Our shuddering limousine carried us southeast for a hundred bruising miles. The asphalt receded, then narrowed, turning first to rough gravel and finally to mud. Gaining light in the cool, cloud-eclipsed dawn, we registered horror out the open window. This eroded countryside had once all been part of the Lacandon Jungle. Tree stumps like tombstones spoke of a forest recently deceased. Here, a ragged battle line for the planet's lungs and pharmacy had been drawn, and nature was plainly losing the war. A century ago only *chicleros* trickled into these woods to mine the slow, rubbery sap of sapodilla trees for Wrigley's gum. Loggers followed, chomping their way through exotic hardwoods right to the jungle's core. Clawing open Eden, they built roads to ease their plunder, let-

Temple of the Sun, Palenque, Mexico

ting loose a flash flood of landless campesinos who slashed and burned their way through the delicate topsoil. Once their cornfields were bled dry, these pioneers were pushed off, bought out, or pressed deeper into the forest by cattle barons whose beef still satisfies First World fast-food cravings. Today we saw these hungry herds on the denuded range, jostling for space with nodding oil rigs and refugees from neighboring countries' bloody civil wars. Together they are devouring this green realm that has for centuries been sanctuary to those legendary Maya people known as the Lacandon.

We knew our escort would belong to this depleted tribe, whose Spanish clerics' epithet—"worshipers of stone"—lends this dwindling forest its name and fame. The Lacandon call themselves the Hach Winik, or True People; for they know they carry the torch passed from the Classic era when their forebears reigned in grandeur at such sites as Bonampak, Palenque, and mighty Tikal. Come the mysterious fall of Classic civilization in the tenth century, Maya culture migrated north, surrendering pyramids and palaces to the rain forest's sultry embrace. A few survivors stayed behind, carrying precious fragments of culture in their hearts. For six hundred years these ancestors of the True People persevered in isolation, fortressed in an island capital at the center of a jungle lake. During the conquest they were joined by other Maya who were fleeing the Spaniards' church and chains. Like stalked animals, the defiant Lacandon remained free but on the run. Building no new pyramids in their wanderings, they instead awakened ancient ones from the jungle hotbed. But the old cities like Bonampak had slept too long in their memory; the Lacandon had forgotten that temple carvings were of kings. And so for centuries these most untouched of the Maya burned their blood and copal incense before stone portraits-turned-to-gods.

Today the Lacandon hover at just a few hundred souls divided between two estranged camps in this besieged forest. Those of the Najá settlement to the north are impenitent "heathens." Exalting the old ways and old colors, these last, true True People roam their forest home barefoot with uncut, unkempt hair and long white cotton tunics. Their recalcitrance is buoyed by Chan K'in Viejo, or "Little Old Sun," their hundred-plus-year-old patriarch, prophet, and bulwark. The southerners of the village of Lacanjá, just sixty miles distant but worlds away, yielded to outside influences in the 1950s, some years after their spiritual leader died unexpectedly of yellow fever, leaving them rudderless. With no one to reveal when to plant, what would cure, or how to beseech the gods, when missionaries descended on the starving Maya with food, fundamentalism, and flashlights, the vulnerable succumbed. Mass conversions, crew cuts, and consumerism followed in quick succession. Lacanjá's succeeding generations now dwell alongside recent forest immigrants who congregate in tiny new assemblies with names like Sinaí, Galilea, Jerusalén, and Paraíso that signal an interloping God and imported hues among the forest's scars.

Scarlet Macaw

Near a small clearing wistfully called Nueva Palestina, our chauffeur dropped us in the mist at the end of a road, vowing he'd be back by dark. We did not have long to wait for our guide, a teenager who popped out of a thatched hut that boasted a fresh bouffant of palm. From the neck down he hailed from the Lacanjá clique: pale blue polyester pants, worn Adidas, and faded "Barcelona '92" T-shirt. But his coppery black hair was pure Najá, savagely long in the style of his northern cousins. "*Yo Sa-ool,*" he mumbled in verbless Spanish; the name, we later gathered, was a Mayan rendition of the biblical Saul. He grasped my arm in an intricate variation on the 1960s soul handshake, so widely and inexplicably adopted by the Maya. In exchange we offered our names and nervous smiles before he turned and plunged into the rain forest at an impressive clip.

Maya trail etiquette called for Sa-ool to lead as senior man, which he was, in jungle savvy if not in years. He gestured for me to follow, thus relegating Sally to the rear, since two could rarely walk abreast. We trotted behind with no hope of keeping pace, just desperate not to lose him. Though this was December, the dry season, here was an endless, stagnant black pool where there should have been a road. Sa-ool splashed right through, knee-deep. With *"no problema"* ringing in our ears, we attempted to skirt the mire and were soon trailing pathetically. Conceding defeat, our guide abandoned the main artery to Bonampak and motioned us off into an uncharted detour.

So here we are, on a hostile path visible only to Sa-ool, scrambling steeply upward, hand-over-hand, then pitching downward, headlong. Encumbered by apparatus and apprehensions, we feel clumsy and unqualified, our educations useless in this green confusion. The forest grants us nothing with which to gauge time, distance, or direction—most certainly not the sun. Without Sa-ool's inner compass pointing the way, even Sally would be utterly adrift. He flows like a shadow, noiseless and graceful, interpreting signs, shapes, and sounds that our senses perceive only as static. We are true *ts'ules,* outsiders.

"Ahoritita" (in a moment), assures Sa-ool. We receive

*House in the Jungle
Nueva Creación,
Chiapas, Mexico*

Casa Flamante
Momostenango, Totonicapán, Guatemala

the same estimate each time we pose the familiar backseat question, "Are we there yet?" Those confident forecasts in Palenque of a two-hour jaunt have dissolved into fable as four grueling hours—and who knows how many miles— pass with no hint of ruins. Our guide stops when he spies an albino termite village looming like an earthen goiter high in a gumbo limbo tree. Later, we all linger to watch a phalanx of black leaf-cutter ants silently parade their green blades aloft, crossing our path to mount the red hill of their colony. We are aware that to the Maya the present is just a comet in endless orbit, spinning from antediluvian past to remotest future and back again. With wristwatches wound to linear time, we also know that today's light is limited— and Bonampak awaits.

This jungle is fat. Trees pile dizzily atop trees against trees in an extravagant cornucopia of redundance. Their bark and branches—whether smooth and pale, prickly, or peeling— all weep fungi, runners, suckers, and the shoots of future giants. An amethyst-colored orchid glances from its nest in a purple sarsaparilla tree studded with

Parrot in Flight

waxy bromeliads, whose lobsterlike spikes are themselves entwined with scarlet passion vines. Renegade philodendrons hold sway over insect-encrusted palms. Wild fuchsia and fiery blooms of the frangipani swoon as if overcome by a breath of their own perfume.

Whenever it is passable, Sa-ool joins the remains of the ancient *sacbé*, or white road. Retracing this ceremonial promenade of Maya kings provokes a chill despite the feverish air. Besides his economical *ahorititas*, he voices fewer than a dozen words along the way. Sign language alone warns of an especially treacherous foothold or thorny spine. The sole sounds accompanying us are the pad of our feet on the musky compost and the liquid birdcalls of some cloistered order sharing only their song.

In this humid hush my mind races. I imagine a time before these imperiled Lacandon abandoned bow and arrow; before the white-skinned, bearded gods with golden hair came floating up in small mountains on the sea; and long before the ancient Maya cities were forsaken to jaguars and jungle spirits. So long ago that even myth does not remember, the Maya "Father-Mothers" crossed the Bering Strait from Asia. Chasing mammoth southward from a "Place of Reeds" through a "Land of Bright Colors" at a pace of just a few miles a decade, they eventually reached Mesoamerica. Here, some four millennia ago, they learned to cultivate their holy corn and built a settled life. Among the region's many evolving cultures, the Olmec were the first to come of age, about a thousand years before Christ. Then, from seminal Olmec yeast, the Maya rose to dominance just five hundred years later. They were not to fall from this pedestal for twenty centuries.

While Europe cowered beneath the shroud of the Dark Ages and Paris was just a rough island village in the Seine, there flowered on this side of the Atlantic a culture with a civilization so brilliant and an architecture so refined as to equal the magnificence of imperial Rome. These were the Classic Maya. Thriving in dozens of rival city-states governed by sage priests and revered kings, they lit up a seven-hundred-year golden age of intellectual, artistic, and spiritual effervescence between A.D. 200 and 900. These Maya toiled, sacrificed, and prayed beneath lavishly painted and ornamented palaces and pyramids. Their constructions—raised without benefit of the wheel, metal tools, or beasts of burden—towered over any building to appear in this hemisphere for a millennium.

Masterful Maya architects, urban planners, and engineers sculpted the landscape as well as their monuments. They sloped plazas to capture precious rain, molded valleys with terraces and dams to harvest crops and fish, and leveled hilltops to open doors for otherworld transactions. Spurred by the primal need to set the clock for planting, Maya stargazers took the pulse of sun and rain and gradually deciphered the intricate heavens. To chronicle the harmonic cadences unfolding in their skies, they perfected mathematics and fashioned writing. Their artists employed this eloquent hieroglyphic script to immortalize Maya elite on building façades and freestanding stones, or stelae. These carved and painted histories proudly proclaimed victories, bloodlines, and new eras.

Color was the Maya's second language, a visual vocabulary embedding creed and custom in its hues like blossoms in amber. Paint was color's alphabet. Brush strokes dripped with meaning. And through the alchemy of Maya hands, polychrome art and architecture—the billboards of their day—spoke with the clarity and impact of a lightning bolt. Together, glyphs and colors allowed the Maya to correspond across distance and time, inscribing a unifying system of tradition and belief uniquely consistent among Native American peoples.

Temples, Tikal, El Petén, Guatemala

"Our colors come from the Beginnings," the Maya say. Long, long ago the creator gods—Itzamná, or Lord Lizard House, and his wife, Ix Chel, or Lady Paintbrush—stretched a measuring cord across the sky and laid out a perfectly square world afloat in a vast, primordial sea. They assigned a cardinal direction and color to each of its four corners. At the very center of this earth, the creators planted a great *yaxché,* or ceiba tree. They colored it *yax,* or blue-green, for all that is precious: life-giving rain, sprouting maize, everlasting jade, and the iridescent plumes of the quetzal bird, which shimmer blue one instant and green the next. This "world tree" flourished. Its branches soared upward through the thirteen levels of the otherworld to hoist the starry arc of heaven. Its roots plunged downward through the nine levels of cold, watery Xibalba to submerge the dreaded underworld. Along the divine *yaxché's* blue-green axis, the ancient gods engaged all three layers of their creation in profound conversation. At the same time, this immense tree thrust open a space for Kinich Ahau—Lord Sun—to set forth upon his blazing rounds and trigger the ticking of time.

To align their new world with the crucial track of the sun, the creators tipped the universe on point. They crowned the east of fiery dawn with *chac,* or red, to reign over the land. Since red blood nourishes Lord Sun and ensures his daily rebirth, great East sets the bearing for Maya sacrifice and prayer. And in the east, cloaked in crimson, dwells the chief Chac, master of all rain-making gods, who to this day barters storm clouds for blood red offerings. Opposite East the gods plotted West and draped it in *ek,* or black, the color of night, death, destruction, and torments of the underworld. Each evening Lord Sun falls into the west to be gobbled up on his dangerous journey through the "inky place of fright." And across black West prowl nine malignant demons and the pitch-black god of war, flashing his obsidian weapons. To either side of Lord Sun's path, the creators spilled their remaining paint pots. Anointing South with *kan,* or yellow, the color of ripe corn and sun's heat at high noon, they entrusted this golden place to the yellow jaguar god of day.

Last of all, they doused North in resplendent *zac,* or white, the color of frosty *nortes,* those north winds that bring rain, Lord Hurakán, and change. And it is from the north that the capricious white goddess of the equinox ushers in a rainbow of new seasons.

Though dulled by millennia, this emblazoned diamond cut by the gods at the dawn of time still softly glints across the Maya lands. More than a physical map of their world, it holds a visual key to Maya belief. Traditional Maya see themselves living on a blue-green island surrounded by the dark blue sea. Each village is thought to sit at the very center of this island, where a blue-green cross—recalling the cruciform *yaxché*—allows the Maya access to gods and ancestors in the other levels of their universe. And like the world, each village aligns itself with the sun on its daily passage from east to west. Just as the sun moves from the red of dawn through the yellow of midday to the black of night through the white of change and back again to the red of dawn, so the Maya see their own lives and the cycle of their corn following this same path from birth to maturity to death through change and back again to rebirth.

At first Sally and I found the Maya map unreadable. After all, our culture orients itself to north and gives little thought to the travels of the sun, much less color meanings. Conditioned to neutrality, our own anemic world knows color mostly as a silenced afterthought, a cosmetic to dress or cover up. But as we traced the afterlife of ancient colors reflecting across the Maya's painted landscape, their enciphered diamond at last gave up its code. To the living Maya, color is not merely a matter of preference but a statement of belief. Color speaks, and its potent dialogue endures.

SUNRISE
EAST

NORTH

SOUTH

WEST
SUNSET

A thunderclap shatters my reverie. High overhead the roaring drumroll of a downpour heralds Noah's flood. There is nowhere to escape the deluge. I check the seal on the plastic wrapped around my camera, and we brace ourselves for rain, but it never comes. We press on, amazed by the forest canopy's sheltering thirst. Twenty minutes later a few hot, colossal drops evade the green umbrella to smack loudly against the ground at our feet. This celestial baptism inspires the joyful chorus we now hear trilling across the emerald dome.

After the storm the midday jungle cooks. The forest's breath hangs weighty and oppressive. An occasional nick in the jungle's skin admits a lean, jaundiced beam where troupes of mosquitoes shimmy in and out of the half-light. We begin to hate this vistaless path of seasonless green that refuses to end. Just when we're afraid that we will take root ourselves, and Sa-ool has embalmed our skepticism with a few more *ahorititas,* we break through a hole in the jungle.

Crossing a shadow line as hard and sharp as a machete's blade, we are instantly blinded. Sunstruck, we sizzle like matches in a white heat that fights with humidity for advantage. Horses graze in this small clearing, hard-won from the forest. Their sweating meadow also passes for an airstrip, though it is just a grassy Band-Aid stuck between

Blue Porch
Abasolo, Chiapas,
Mexico

Callejon El Calvario
Oaxaca, Mexico

enormous, buttressed trees. Sally stops to contemplate this rutted runway and sighs with relief that flight had not been an alternative. Then I spot the three-wheeled, all-terrain motorcycle that had been guaranteed as our way out in an emergency. Ominously crippled by rust and weeds, and obviously long out of service and fuel, it will come to no one's rescue.

At a trio of meager huts a young Maya guard invites us in and softly asks in halting Spanish that we sign his scratch-pad registry. Overlook his sweat-stained Pepsi cap and updated clothes, and he is wrenched right off a Maya carving. His broad, flat forehead slopes to meet a long, elegantly hooked nose, and high cheekbones frame large, epicanthic eyes. This caretaker seems pleased that we have broken the monotony of his shift. He says he is new, just five months at his post, working thirty days straight, followed by a dozen off to visit his wife and child. In a busy week, he admits, he may greet only half a dozen hikers. Lack of fresh logbook entries confirms his stint in solitary.

Emerging from the respite of his thatched outpost, Sally and I spot a rainbow pinching the site within its incandescent arc. "*Yax, kan, chac,* it is the tail feathers of a macaw," volunteers the guard for our benefit. Sa-ool, unexpectedly possessive, says that to the Lacandon, the rainbow is Ah Shuki, who burns the clouds away with fire. The two teens then lean into the shade of a spreading breadnut tree to trade stories as best they can in the muted clucks and shushes of kindred Mayan tongues. As they idle, Sa-ool examines bits of broken stone. I wonder if this casual act unconsciously recalls the days, only a generation ago, when the Lacandon still journeyed to this home of the gods to gather pebbles. They

Stela Detail, Bonampak, Mexico

would burn these sacred stones with incense, bidding sylvan deities to come listen to their prayers. The Maya regard an ancient site like Bonampak as we might a beach house shut up for winter season. It still has an owner. Desolation and peeling paint are only temporary. Life will return when time circles back.

A few crumpled stone boxes poke gap-toothed from atop a stepped green hill riddled with stairs, stelae, terraces, and altars, forming one squat pyramid. So this is Bonampak, "City of Painted Walls," the paltry remains of a small, late-Classic center under the thumb of the nearby city of Yaxchilán. I try to picture what this place must have looked like so many centuries ago at its frescoes' genesis. Just like the sacred architecture of classical Greece, whose familiar white marble was originally adorned in flamboyant colors, these gray stones before us also once dazzled in a riot of powerful hues. But sun, rain, and forest tentacles have stripped them naked, plundering all but the flecks we still find clinging to the walls.

Maya pyramids, plazas, and indeed whole cities like Bonampak were once lovingly painted inside and out. As the Maya reckoned it, the gods gave colors to living things like flowers, flesh, trees, and birds. When these died, the gods took their colors away, bleaching all to the white of bones and corn husks. And so it followed for the Maya to clone the colors of the living to bring their sacred, bare-stone cities to life, just as they animate their painted villages today.

Most ancient Maya centers were awash in red paint, the color of sacrifice. It was as if spilled blood were pouring off engorged altars, spurting out temple doors, and gushing down pyramid steps to soak plazas with this vital sustenance that kept the sun rising and corn sprouting. But why would red initiate rebirth? At the dawn of Creation, the deities offered their own divine blood mixed with corn paste to create the Maya people. So red blood is the gods' property, their thirst-quenching drink and best-loved bribe for services rendered. Royal blood was most cherished of all, an open artery to otherworlds. The gods could always be counted on to swap their rain for the king's shed blood.

For the Maya there is no free lunch. Long ago they struck a bargain with their gods: rain, health, victory, and ample harvest in exchange for blood offerings and lavish praise. Just as coursing blood nourishes people, so rain—the sky's shed blood—feeds the earth. Hence red blood, through sacrifice, becomes water. Fire, which to the Maya is just as volatile as blood, serves as the catalyst for this transfusion. When red blood spattered on incense is set afire, yellow flames and black smoke join with those from burning maize fields to curl into the blue heavens, beckoning the gods and seeding black clouds. These burst forth, spilling precious blue rain, which feeds the yellow seed corn buried within the black earth. From out of this underworld death, the kernels soon sprout the rich green of new life to yield more yellow corn. The fields then die and bleach to white, and so it goes. Blood and fire, filtering upward to the gods, ensure that water will flow downward from the gods in an unbroken circle of propitiation and precipitation. Thus through the cycle of sustaining corn, the Maya and their gods are bound in holy covenant to maintain cosmic balance. Once-sanguine Bonampak was securely tethered to this ever-pulsing color wheel of renewal.

The jungle's claws have barely been clipped since this site was first disclosed to white men in 1946. That year, draftsman John Bourne and draft resister Carl Frey, two American adventurers living among the Lacandon, were led to these ruins by one of their Maya friends. They just missed the murals, whose temple was masked in undergrowth. Their guide soon died from snakebite: retribution, his people assessed, for revealing this hallowed place. Four months later, while filming the Lacandon for the jungle giant United Fruit Company, photographer Giles Healey became the first outsider to enter the dripping sanctuary and gaze upon the phenomenal paintings. He reported that the hidden galleries, still pungent with the resinous tang of recent copal offerings, were betrayed by a black puma exiting its painted lair. His provocative find spawned jealousy, death, accusation, and uproar as governments, explorers, and institutions each staked their claims. The most intriguing tale stars Frey. Assuming the name Carlos, he was championed by Mexico as a native son and modern-day Columbus before he drowned on expedition. His exploits among the ruins sparked a ballet, a novel, and even a *Cosmo* feature on his Lacandon mistress, Margarita. Fascination with Bonampak remains just as intense today. In fact, for nearly a decade our own project has been inspired by descriptions of the murals' pivotal hues.

Like acolytes drawn to a shrine, Sally and I ignore the distractions of the stunted, paint-stripped acropolis. We ascend only as far as the three humble doorways in a small, simple building so majestically christened Structure 1. A halo of sunlight illuminates the broken shell, refuge of the cherished murals. We are awed that just beyond these portals lie the only intact Classic Maya wall paintings, and we are stunned that this temple—its roof crest fallen—seems defenseless against villains of weather and wildlife save for a corrugated cap of tin and three pathetic screen gratings. But miraculously, at Bonampak, enemy has proven savior. Faulty construction and more than a thousand rainy seasons admitted a slow trickle of water through fissured vaults. This frosted the masterpiece in a thin glaze of lime that sealed out centuries of incense, insects, animals, light, and moisture. New threats to the colors crescendoed with this century's rediscovery. Suddenly Bonampak became a bull's-eye for looters and a practice range for off-the-mark conservationists, all the while dodging bullets of regional unrest. Against incalculable odds, the murals survived. Recently, an expert preservation team cast off the calcium shield, at long last liberating the colors' original brilliance and import.

No book's description could have prepared us for the wonders unfolding across the temple's inner walls. Its three cells are flooded with astonishingly fresh, vital colors. Entering the first chamber, we are swept up in a raucous spectacle profiled against a rich turquoise blue seemingly borrowed from the butterflies that have drifted in and out of our morning. Entranced dancers spin and sway, bedecked in opulent brocades and sporting wings of vivid blue-green plumage. Gyrating celebrants surge past in grotesque costumes mimicking aquatic underworld deities. Rapt musicians encircle us, their fanfare caught in midnote. We can almost hear the hypnotic chant of gourd rattles and the moan of conch-shell trumpets; the metered scratch of bone rasps and the staccato clatter of antler on carapace; the throb of a great wooden drum and the low lament of long, bleating horns. With crimson seashell brooches or regal jade at their throats, Maya nobles orchestrate this mystical procession, their red-stained bodies arrayed in yellow jaguar skins or elegant finery embroidered in tropical hues. Presiding over all, florid gods nod approval from on high.

Moving into the center room, we cringe as a ferocious battle leaps off sumptuous walls of forest green and celestial blue. Grimacing warriors dyed the potent red of blood or the black of war violently twist, writhe, and lunge in a brutal jumble of hand-to-hand combat. Flint-tipped lances snap. Shields and body parts fly. Clubs swing as trumpets herald. The vanquished are dragged by their hair from the chaos and paraded into a scene of severed heads, torn fingernails, and dripping blood. Readied for sacrifice, humiliated captives stripped of clothes and color beg for mercy as they are draped across blood red pyramid steps, the very ones we climbed to reach this spot.

The final vault breathes life into boisterous victory festivities. Its walls seem to vibrate with luxuriant dance and music—a remittance for the gods' rewards. Like resplendent peacocks, royal priests flourishing massive, feathered headgear and intensely patterned capes strut across this same red

pyramid. One brandishes an obsidian knife poised to plunge into the outstretched flesh of a bound sacrificial victim. In counterpoint, white-robed noblewomen seated upon a green table set with red disks casually pierce their tongues to donate blood in execution of exalted duty.

These late-eighth-century murals recite three chapters in the contemporaneous epic of Bonampak's final dynasty under Chaan Muan, or Lord Sky Bird Celestial God; his wife Yax Conejo, Lady First Green Rabbit; and their child, who was destined to be the last male heir. This scion is presented to the royal court in the first room. In the second, vessels of blood are gathered in his honor. In the third, this blood is spilled, which gains the gods' authority and favor for the young successor while it brings the painted temple to life. The baby prince protagonist is all but lost to us among some three hundred near-life-size characters populating the thick walls. It is only semiotic colors that help us negotiate the crowd, signaling who's who and what's what like murmured passwords.

Drawn back to the first room's pageant, I envision a royal artist-scribe setting about his sacred task. Born to his calling and rigorously trained, he now provides access to the will of the gods and their cosmic cycle through metaphoric color. For weeks he has remained ritually purified, as has this sanctuary. Clouds of incense hang heavily in the air. The chamber bustles with activity. Exhausted plasterers, dusted in white from the morning's fevered tempo, clean their wooden trowels and stone burnishers. Their hands are cracked from the caustic batter of burned lime, sand, water, and retardant tree sap. The artist has just finished transferring a set of his bark-paper portraits and patterns into the smooth, wet walls with a bone point. Now, with seashell palette and badger-tail brush in hand, he stands atop the low bench that runs around the room and applies bold colors to clarify the symbols and call out the rank of all he has just sketched. Dedicated apprentices, glistening with sweat, fill in the large fields with solid color, throwing paint onto the raw surface with forceful strokes. Meanwhile, anticipating their master's needs, harried assistants rhythmically scrape flint spatulas against shallow stone mortars. Grinding pigments into pastes, they prepare white from burned limestone; black from charcoal or burned bone; and reds ranging from dark orange, umber, and magenta to scarce, glittering scarlet, all quarried from the rusty earth.

The artist, intent on distinguishing a jaguar-skin breechcloth, orders up more rare yellow. Using a recipe known by heart, his protégé scoops hydrated iron oxide

cakes of permanent dye. Diluting the prized color chips, he climbs wooden scaffolding high into the corbeled arch to sweep sapphire blue scrolls across the commanding masks of gods, earning their patronage while sealing their divine identity.

Just on the verge of completing his holy commission, the esteemed artist must have dropped his brush in mid-stroke and run. These murals were never finished. The

Musician

Battle

Nobles

into a clay bowl and stirs in a bit of crushed charcoal, a dash of warming red ocher, water, and a touch of plant juice or human blood as binder. Working swiftly with this golden slurry, the master makes every motion count. As his strokes dry, the pigments fuse to the wall in true fresco. The painter moves on. He breaks off nuggets of precious Maya blue, a complex concoction of a special clay and fermented indigo that has been boiled, dried, and formed into small

glyphic name of the boy-who-would-be-king was never painted on its panel, and the child did not ascend to this or any throne. Bonampak and so many other cities were abandoned. The Maya dispersed, their Classic culture eclipsed; and painting of such realism and power disappeared from the ancient Americas forever. We may never know what throttled these Maya. Perhaps their once-ritualized skirmishes metastasized into bloody and destructive wars. It could have been plague, pestilence, or peasant revolt, coupled with an earthquake, volcanic eruption, or crazed king. No doubt the Maya building boom and overpopulation leveled forests for mortar and fuel. This possibly disrupted regular rains and thus the sacred cycle of renewal. Without roots to hold the depleted soil, when rain did fall rivers would have run red with the blood of the fields, and famine would have chased the Maya from this land. But all we really know for certain is that by the tenth century, Classic cities like Bonampak were built and painted no more. Most of the surviving Maya regrouped into squabbling states in the Yucatán. Over the next six centuries their widespread trade routes and cultural exchange set the stage for central Mexico's great Toltec and Aztec empires. But these were all to crumble with the anchoring of the Spaniards, who found meaning in only one color: gold.

Sa-ool hails us in Mayan from the plaza. Three hours of photographing have melted away, and Bonampak's stones now hang in afternoon shadow. Sally and I wind our way down the rough steps past the great carved stela, which was ritually broken when the Classic Maya fled. Stopping off at the guard's hut, we buy a round of warm *refrescos,* which have been stored, for appearances only, in the carcass of a gas refrigerator. When Sa-ool nonchalantly brushes a hairy tarantula the size of my fist off the hand-hewn bench, I watch Sally mentally add arachnids to her inventory of potential perils. Diverting her own attention, she admires our guide's long tangle of hair and teases that his name should be Samson, not Saul. "Well, it makes me strong too," he replies, confirming that he's heard the missionaries' stories. Returning the compliment, he praises Sally's teeth, "like kernels of white seed corn." Encouraged by this verbal advance, Sally doffs her baseball cap to reveal a nearly shaved head. This haircut-gone-awry astonishes Sa-ool and the guard, prompting much discussion. Suddenly Sa-ool points out the sun's position and warns, "Our Father goes. Soon the red-eyed spirits come." Sally's homeward litany of terrors has just lengthened: snakes, spines, spiders, and now

lurking spirits, too. With great reluctance we take our leave of the custodian and his murals and fall back into the gaping green mouth of the monster.

The sun's swift progress further loosens Sa-ool's tongue. Since Spanish is a second language for all of us, we are oral equals. Sally and I must struggle to fathom Mayañol, our guide's Spanish sprinkled with Mayan; but our curiosity, bottled up after hours of silence, hurdles this barrier as Sa-ool weaves Maya history, legend, and dreams into tales from his life and forest world. *"Pues entonces"* (well then), he begins; for this is how he opens each new thought, liberally sprinkling in *bueno* (good) and *mire* (look here) as punctuation. *"Pues entonces,* my grandfather was born in the time of fever, the son of a jaguar of the darkness. Everyone feared I was a jaguar too; because when I was small, my mother had dreams. Yes, spots came on my legs, *mire,* on all my body." Moving his eyes from side to side, he crouches, growls, and claws the air before concluding, *"Pues, bueno,* I was healed. I was dipped in a big pot of green and red chilies. I remember it burned. But the spots, *entonces,* listen up, they burned away."

Slowing his stride, Sa-ool sheds the last of his shyness. *"Pues entonces,* before the missionaries, before the road, *pues,* there was a big battle here, yes, right here. Not a little one," he belabors, spreading open his hands. *"Mire,* it was big when the *mexicanos* came with many guns to kill us. We were not afraid. Then, back then, our gods had power, though my people had only bows and arrows. Our gods, *pues,* they live nearby, and they hear us. They made the soldiers' guns shoot water, only water," he says with a laugh, aiming a make-believe rifle. "And the strangers' gods, *pues bueno,* they live on the other side of a great lake where there are big mountains, at least three days away by boat, far away. Their gods could not hear their cries; and, *pues entonces,* my people, they made them die with long arrows. Soldiers never came again." Sa-ool's story is typically Maya. Slipping in a little personal commentary, he tangles fact and fiction like jungle roots, with events ordered by importance,

Woven Bag and Crucifix
Zacualpa, El Quiché,
Guatemala

Cuatro Colores
Chichicastenango, El Quiché, Guatemala

Embroiderer's Hands
San Mateo Ixtatán, Huehuetenango, Guatemala

not date, and players interchangeable. Was this the time of the Spanish Conquest, Mexican Revolution, or arrival of the loggers? Just when, he cannot say, but it doesn't really matter, since the Maya present has breathed in the past and will live again in the future. What counts is that the Maya and their gods prevail and that the old ways triumph over new.

As if an alarm has sounded through the jungle, it is four o'clock: the hour that insects and birds dance their daily tango. King-size or peewee, lacy or armored, our antennaed enemies buzz, bite, spit, whir, hum, hiss, drone, click, crawl, and tick, driving us mad and ever more quickly onward. Our airborne defense team arrives in one big squawking, screeching flutter and soon drowns out the entomological chorus with a colorful avian opera. Booming hoots and frantic whistles shower down, along with pieces of fruit and branches, as birds wheel about in feeding frenzy. Sa-ool effortlessly mimics their warbles, sobs, and arpeggios, though we rarely catch a glimpse of the blue wing or yellow breast that responds. We soon have ringside seats as spider monkeys perform their high-wire act. They startle a flock of rainbow-billed toucans dining in a ramon nut tree who skitter off, dragging their tremendous beaks. We are startled in turn by the machine-gun outburst of a *chachalaca* bird who heckles two lipstick-red-headed parrots bickering over sapodilla plums. Sa-ool retrieves some of their scattered treats, offering us the soft yellow pulp and certifying, *"Pues entonces,* full moon makes it very sweet."

As we plod along, Sa-ool patiently catalogs the forest. "This bush gives red dye like blood," he says, "and that vine, fresh water. We twist this bark to make good hammocks, and that leaf is medicine for headache," which he

Blue-Fronted Parrot

mimes by pounding his temple. *"Pues entonces,* there is a man in the forest made all of plants," Sa-ool maintains. "All green, *bueno,* you believe he is a man. But when you cut him, he heals himself." Amused by Sally's scribblings whenever we slow down, he confides, *"Pues entonces, bueno,* a healer, he used a wand made of this palm and a blue stone to heal me. Listen up, he healed me with a green wand when I had a turtle in my stomach." With these tales Sally records yet more flashbacks to the redemptive power of *yax.*

When I ask Sa-ool what's needed to build a house, he obliges and soon tags one tree for rafters and another for corner posts, "straight, yes, and strong as stone in the earth." He also identifies three types of palm fronds for roof thatch. With interlaced fingers he models how these are double-woven against rain. "And this vine, made soft with water, ties our house together, *mire,* it dries strong," he asserts with a clenched fist. Reverentially patting the bronze mast of a fledgling mahogany, or *ka'wakché,* as he instructs, Sa-ool tells us that it could one day yield two canoes, "but, *entonces,* we no longer hollow them with fire and with ax. *Mire,* now we go in buses." Then he motions to a sapodilla, source of the hard, heavy timber that still survives in Classic-era lintels. Its trunk bears old scars from a *chiclero's* knife. *"Bandito,"* he judges. *"Pues entonces,* you know, you must ask forgiveness when you cut a tree. *Mire,* you must receive permission. *Pues entonces, mire,* they bleed like us. They die. Yes, so many die now. They are gone, hear me, and there is little to hunt." Sally and I sense that Sa-ool's forest code is the very same foundation of reciprocity upon which the great Maya pyramids were built, now cycled back and pared down to essentials.

Growing troubled, our animist escort tracks the waning light and waxing stillness of evening's fall. He urges us to hurry before the sun no longer protects the world and the forest turns wild and evil. That's when the beasts with *ojos rojos* (red eyes) stalk the trails, devouring slackers for supper and returning satiated to the underworld at dawn. *"Pues entonces,* first you hear the trees move, then you feel a hot breath, then, *mire,* you see their red eyes glowing like fire," Sa-ool cautions with foreboding. *"Pues entonces,* you can only hide or fight with arrows." He stiffens, pausing to listen for their rustle.

The darkness pulses with small, strange sounds. We feel increasingly vulnerable. "Do Zapatistas roam this part of the jungle?" we probe. *"Pues entonces,* who knows?" he replies, shrugging mysteriously. Just then Sally and I jump and duck when high above our heads a sagging limb creaks beneath the weight of a dark shape that lets out a labored wheeze and anguished scream, climaxed by a deafening roar. Sa-ool grins and soothes, *"Pues entonces, bueno,* only howler monkeys." But a few minutes later, when some creature comes crashing

Ritual Celebrant, Bonampak, Mexico

through the underbrush and we freeze, even Sa-ool is spooked. Waving a hand to silence us, he reads fresh tracks in the mud and a patch of stiff hairs snagged on some bark. With a low snort and grunt he conjures some entity we're too tired to even guess. We move mechanically, dropping one foot before the other while tree frogs croak the beat. Though my watch tells me there should still be daylight in Chiapas, here it has been leached by the canopy. Feeling our way like the blind, we now know why these Maya speak of walking "under the forest."

In the anonymity of this underworld darkness, I ask Sa-ool about his beliefs. At first he declares that he has no faith at all, but soon he confesses, *"Pues entonces,* our people spoke with the gods at Bonampak, yes, and at Yaxchilán, too. My father's father, *pues bueno,* he tells me of those days. But my father no longer makes the journey, *mire,* he burns no copal, no blood. *Pues,* he is *evangélico.* He says Hachäkyum, Our True Lord, is gone. *Pues, mire,* his new God can read and write. I see His black book, I hear His songs. But I do not know. The old gods built the old cities, *pues entonces,* these places are still their home." And so this skeptical Saul is no New Testament Paul, at least not yet. With his long locks and running shoes he spans two worlds and several thousand years, at once reliquary of ancient legacy and catchall for the dubious new.

The distance widens between weary Sally, lagging far behind, and hungry Sa-ool, pace ever quickening. Just when I hear him declare, "The stomach asks for tortillas," we reach his edge of the jungle. We have foiled the *ojos rojos!* Dragging ourselves across the clearing to Sa-ool's family compound, we pass half a dozen huts impersonating the huge, fragile nests of some prehistoric bird. The rustic courtyard is littered with scrawny chickens, burned patches, clay pots, a purple plastic bucket, and an old dugout canoe serving as a trough for two pigs. Just beyond we spot the contused van and a fidgety Carlos in the calamine pink twilight. To our sore eyes and bodies the rolling wreckage is now a luxury sedan, and our driver the perfect host as he slices up sweet, dripping chunks of fresh pineapple. I heartily thank Sa-ool and shake his hand once more, while Sally and one of his plaid-skirted sisters make an exchange: my wife's favorite glass-beaded bracelet for two strands of blue, yellow, and white plastic gems strung with red and black jungle seeds.

With the Maya color cosmos encircling our wrists, we bump and bounce our way back to Palenque. The radio long gone to glory, resilient Carlos whistles merrily as though nothing in the world could go wrong. A bat launches through our headlights and into the night. Constellations of fireflies twinkle messages to the stars. At the final checkpoint before town, in one of those surreal moments of waking life, boy soldiers smile and wave us through upon a languid breeze bearing the fragrance of vanilla and the exquisite strains of an unfamiliar aria.

Graceless Palenque now looks downright dapper. I check my camera, and it's still conscious, but our shoes will never be the same. Neither will we. Hot water is not to be had to soothe our stiffening bodies, but cold showers do much to calm our stings and scratches. Before we fall asleep, I calculate and am amazed to discover that our first contact with the murals comes exactly 1,204 years to the day since Bonampak's young heir debuted before royal society on December 14, 790. Our rest is fitful. That night, and many nights thereafter, we dream of this extraordinary passage and demons with fiery red eyes.

Blue Ossuary
Tenabo, Campeche, Mexico

Hammock
Río Lagartos, Yucatán, Mexico

2
PAINTED HOUSES
BURNING BRIGHT AS CANDLES

"How many valleys away is your home, and does corn grow there?" inquires old Sebastián, pressing his end of a measuring cord to the base of the freshly laid adobe wall. At the other end of the string, from high atop a rough ladder, his youngest son, Pedro, checks the height of a ridgepole saddle and cranes to hear my reply. Our Maya house-building host, who has patiently indulged our curiosity all morning on this hillside lot, poses the customary question here in the mountains of San Lorenzo Zinacantan, Chiapas. It is the very same question asked in the Lacandon Jungle and all across the Maya world, for the Maya are known as the People of the Corn. Corn, or maize, is the foundation of their culture. Corn fills their talk, their prayers, their bellies, and their days. So I am glad my Indiana roots grant an answer with

Rainy Season
Xela, Quezaltenango, Guatemala

OPPOSITE
Maya House Relief, Uxmal, Yucatán, Mexico

which we can all identify: "I come from many, many valleys away, beyond Mexico, beyond Texas, from a place with much ice and snow. And yes, we have corn, much corn. In summer the land is green as far as the eye can see, and yellow mountains rise with harvest."

The Maya can truly say they are what they eat. They believe that the gods first molded them from ground maize; and ever since, corn has been their sustenance from sunrise to sunset, birth to death. To plant corn, or "make *milpa,*" and bring forth golden *gracia,* or "divine grace," is to live. Corn's cycle, from which the very name *Maya* derives, orders their year more surely than our seasons. Care of maize in the field is man's sacred duty, just as its preparation at the hearth is woman's. Shirking their shared covenant with the gods would invite more than starvation and disgrace. This breach would throw Our Father Sun off course, severing the timeless round of sacrifice, burning, planting, rain, and harvest, and etiolating the cycle's red, black, green, blue, and yellow to white, the absence of all color.

"Good heart" is key when building a house, the highland Maya say. Since Sally and I emit no ill will, the good-hearted let us watch. Sebastián—plumed in the woven, pink-striped, pompon-swinging poncho, white shorts, and leather sandals that are an elder Zinacanteco's everyday regalia—tells of the hundreds of sunbaked bricks required to rear these thick walls for Pedro and his young wife. "My son is ripe and needs his own home," he explains. Pedro, blushing to match his own tasseled pink tunic worn atop a snazzy chartreuse shirt, blue jeans, and work boots, points out the pit, now cracked and dry, where his building blocks were cast. He recounts how, at the end of the rains, he dug moist red

Seed Corn, Zinacantan, Mexico

clay away from the perimeter of the house site. This left behind a ten-by-fifteen-foot raised area that is now earthen floor for this typical one-room home. "The adobe will not crack," he asserts. "We mix in long needles of the forest pines." The walls are mortared with this same mud, and Pedro demonstrates how he will butter them with mud plaster before painting. "*Kan,* I think. Yellow, like a dog." "A dog?" I puzzle. "Yes, a dog. I like yellow. And I will have a roof of tile, not grass like the old houses."

A spanking new house, ritzy roof, and yellow paint job too? In the Maya world any one of these could incite whispers of "too much money" or "too little shared" and arouse dreaded envy. Then nightmare visits from witches sent by jealous neighbors would lead to "soul loss," illness, or even death. Like his pre-Columbian shadow, today's Maya is both goaded and guided by the stick of envy in tandem with the carrot of respect that comes by way of *cargo,* or community service. *Cargo*—literally the load borne for the common good—values the village over the individual in every kernel of daily life. Within its elaborate system of rotating obligations, the Maya find worth and purpose through their shared "burden" to honor gods, saints, ancestors, and holy corn. Those who serve with "good heart" over the course of a lifetime reap prestige and a "warm soul" in return.

Together the social glues of envy and *cargo* maintain collective health and harmony, ideally balancing all to a perfect standstill. To the Maya, "keeping up with the Joneses" means exactly that. Do not exceed or excel in any way. Safeguard with sameness. And to lessen liability if prosperity should threaten, take out a blanket insurance policy: invest all surplus in public sites and ceremonies through

Earthen House
Agua Alegre, Huehuetenango, Guatemala

cargo. Any action not scrupulously faithful to these leveling forces imperils the communal heart and endangers one's soul. Foolhardy Maya who flaunt good fortune or dare to be different take a great risk. Even house paint can be hazardous, for it is extravagant and sets neighbors apart.

The Mexicans have a proverb, "If envy were paint, the whole world would be painted." Traditional Maya are well aware of envy's long reach. In defense, most paint little of their personal domain. This leaves whole villages of whitewashed or bare mud houses. But even where a lone brightly colored home would stand out as a reckless act, there is always paint elsewhere in town. Like the temples and tombs of old, Maya churches and cemeteries are alive with color. This public paint glorifies not mortals but the gods, saints, and ancestors who are the source of community well-being. Such painting—whether in the name of *cargo* or the dead—cannot invoke envy.

Given envy's power, it might seem that this book should hold no chapter on painted Maya houses, but a transition is in progress. As Sally and I scan the valley of Zinacantan, we note that the *na,* or traditional house of thatched wattle and daub still found throughout the highlands, will soon lose out to tiled adobes. Paint's approval rating is also on the rise. It is at the hazardous intersections where the murmur of the village meets the clamor of the modern world that we find residential color. As change chips away at old ways, the fear of envy calms. There is safety in numbers; so even here in traditional Zinacantan, Pedro is not imprudent in his canine yellow dream.

No matter who actually lives in them, the painted houses in changing villages are branded by Maya as *ladino*

Painted Entry, San Antonio Sacatepéquez, Guatemala

style, or latinized. *Ladinos*—whether mestizos or people of pure native blood—prize family and nation over village. They have abandoned traditional languages, clothing, and customs, including restraints on house paint. Though *ladino* and Maya may live side by side, their beliefs, values, hopes, and fears reside on opposite ends of the earth. Maya like Pedro, who risk painting their house, agree that change must come with consensus or not at all. They take great care to keep within the protective bounds of envy evasion and *cargo*. *Ladino* incentives could not be more alien, taking their cues from Old World ambitions that arrived with the Spanish. Just as in Spain, even the simplest stucco house of a *ladino* swaggers in its opulent coat of colors. It feigns wealth with bands of paint that counterfeit the coveted cut stone its owners cannot afford around windows, doors, and the lower wall so vulnerable to sheep and soccer balls. Employing paint on the street side only for greatest impact, a *ladino*'s house cries out for attention with ostentatious hues. An engraved invitation to witches? This is hardly a *ladino*'s concern. He strives to make neighbors jealous of his genius and riches.

Maya and *ladino* motives are not the only governors of color; another impulse is at play. I recall the afternoon this truth was driven home to us in the city of Valladolid in Mexico's Yucatán State, where we spoke with a *ladina* Maya mother of six sons. "We paint because we love color," she said. "You see, my neighbor has three colors. I have painted my own house with four. And my door, it is the blue of the sea." Moments later, as I genuflected mid-road to photograph her exuberant pastiche of Old and New World colors, an executive behind the wheel of his steel gray Mercedes nearly ran me down. Stopping to apologize, the upper-class businessman laughed at my subject. "Such shrill colors, they are gaudy," he declared. "The painters must have crickets in their heads." Holding to a highbrow preference for pristine white—the choice of Spain's elite—he was unaware of the irony that white is also the only house color of the poorest, most tradition-bound Maya.

Squawks and gobbles call us back to the construction zone, where Pedro shoos turkeys off a stockpile of future rafters and frees the largest timber. "It is the head," Sebastián defines. Muscular thighs straining, he accepts my offer to help tilt this heavy ridgepole into place. Like all the wood, it is just a machete-stripped tree trunk; there are no lumberyards in a Maya village. Instead, builders must await the days of the full—or "ripe"—moon. Only then are plants and trees mature enough to volunteer for the job; it is said they can be heard pledging not to split, break, or rot. During monthly lunar lustiness, villages bustle as corn is planted, crops harvested, babies conceived, and saplings felled for furniture and

Red Surround, Valladolid, Mexico

framing. I am told that the "roofing crew" will soon return in a borrowed truck from the city of San Cristóbal de las Casas, closest source of precious fired tiles. These friends and relatives form a skilled labor bank where all villagers deposit and withdraw. A man might build himself two houses in a lifetime; but he will assist with many more from the time he is a boy, digging holes and steadying logs. Like Amish at a barn raising, workers are paid in food, drink, and the assurance that hands will be there for them one day.

After struggling with the beam, we stand back to admire the progress. I ask what determined the house site.

"A priest, a shaman," Pedro cautiously discloses, wiping his brow on a frayed bandanna. "But why does it sit at an odd angle to the road?" I pursue. Sebastián's brown arm sweeps across the sky until it reaches the sun in a simple gesture with profound meaning. At once I understand. The ridgepole aligns with this sacred track rather than with the dirt path of least resistance up the hill. Our Father Sun still dominates this valley, and ears of corn are still his "holy sunbeams." By seating this house along the sun's journey, Pedro confirms the harmony of the universe and his own ordered part in it. Soon a sacrifice will be offered in the center of the earthen floor, a three-stone hearth will be laid in the west, and an altar will rise in the powerful east, where moon, stars, and rain clouds also dawn. The entrance will always face south to the warming strength of the sun. But I wonder how long this home will be able to keep its back to El Norte, to change.

Another lesson among dozens in our widespread course on Maya house building concludes when five ruddy-cheeked women and girls arrive in a whirl of pink cloth trimmed and tufted in lilacs, yellows, and limes. Barefoot despite the mountain cold, they command the misty landscape with their colors. As they unwrap tortillas from gorgeous woven cloths and dish up steaming black beans from a dented pot, they are all smiles and questions for their men, who explain our presence in soft, birdlike tones. I ask to photograph the house before we leave. Conferring with Sebastián, Pedro declines with, "Perhaps another day, when it is standing. In a week or two. But now it is too tender."

Poised on this grassy, boulder-strewn hill, we are overshadowed by volcanic ridges blanketed in lush forests of

*Carpenter's House
Chuina, Campeche,
Mexico*

Two Red Chairs
San Cristóbal de las Casas,
Chiapas, Mexico

oak and pine. Below us lies an eroded basin of small, terraced cornfields, orchards, and greenhouses, crisscrossed by thin, rusty paths. These all lead down into Zinacantan, the civil and ceremonial center for some 30,000 Tzotzil-speaking Maya who live scattered across the serrated western edge of highland Chiapas. Though situated just a few miles from the *ladino* bastion of San Cristóbal and sliced by the Pan American Highway, which carries the twentieth century right past its door, Zinacantan still clings fiercely to old ways. A few innovations are tolerated, however, including new fertilizers that empower the tired red soil to yield sacred corn, thus ensuring that here the color-soaked cycle will not stall.

On the valley floor below, Sally and I can make out remnants of the Spanish town grid foisted upon all Maya after the conquest. Fresh from hard-won triumph over the Moors, Spaniards applied their same convert-or-die formula to the New World. To ease the saving of Maya souls, the conquerors decreed that the entire Maya way of life must end. After burning down scattered hamlets, they herded the populace into new, Spanish-style towns that were based on Renaissance plans and built atop the ruins of Maya ceremonial centers. However, the Spaniards' refined urban blueprint—just like the Catholicism it escorted—caught on only where it overlapped with Maya traditions. Similarities, in fact, are striking. Ancient Maya plazas survive in today's central square, still the heart of civic and religious life and site of regular markets. This square is flanked by painted church and town hall, stand-ins for temple-pyramid and palace. And just like their colorful ancient counterparts, painted shops and the houses of esteemed *cargo* officials extend outward from the square

Juan's House, San Antonio Palopó, Guatemala

to the four cardinal directions on a lattice of short spurs. Beyond this, today as long ago, order quickly dissolves into a haphazard sprawl of simple family compounds.

The Maya had good reason to resist Spanish plans. Natives who did not fall prey to the assassin squad of European epidemics that raced just ahead of the conquistadors were often ambushed by these raging diseases when jammed into the ordained town grid. Besides, the Maya had long held to a more meaningful order of their own, based on their diamond map, which divided the earth into color-filled quadrants and sacred center. The Maya also distinguished between tame and wild realms. The wild was savage chaos, creatured by ferocious animals and demons; it once covered all the world. The first Maya took portions of this lawless, wooded expanse and transformed them into square plots of safe, civilized space— the tame—like villages and cornfields, where the gods were continually placated. The wild still harbors earth's most holy landmarks: mountains climbing into the heavens; caves opening onto the underworld; and forests—the gardens of the gods—whose branches and roots link all three domains. To maintain communion with the otherworlds, preconquest Maya replicated the hallowed features of the wilds within the tamed refuge of their cities. A pyramid was a sacred mountain; its temple entrance, a consecrated cave. Groups of temples formed exalted mountain ranges overlooking open plazas. These plazas were planted with forests of blessed stelae, or *te tun* (tree stones), which served as divine *yaxché*. And to amplify sanctity while engendering life, this built landscape was painted.

Today's Maya views his village and all it contains in precisely the same way: as a sacrosanct, cultivated enclave

Painted Arcade
Tlacotalpan, Veracruz, Mexico

secure from the barbarous. His house is a model of the gentle village, with its protective orientation and four walls fencing out the wild. Its peaked roof is a holy mountain, and its door, a cavelike entry to the underworld, which lies beneath its earthen floor. Much that is made by human hands recalls both village and house as squares of tamed, propitiated space: the cemetery with its forest of crosses and its tombs with their dark, cavelike niches; the church and its altars; beds and tables; and even woven cloth. No matter that houses are rectangular, that cornfields now veer far from square, that conquistadors have chopped down the sacred *yaxché* at village center, or that the four cardinal roads into town sometimes number seven and run at skewed angles. The Maya still chart their world from the ancient diamond with its five symbolic hues.

Sanctuary extends only to village edge. Mexico City is well beyond these bounds, and the United States, lord only knows. Since Sally and I descend from the unknown wilds, far from Zinacantan's "navel," locals—like the rosy line padding downhill behind us—tend to keep their distance. Despite their heavy loads of firewood, they scurry past on mud-caked feet, impervious to the sharp stones. Suddenly we are adrift in a sea of black wool as a young shepherdess hurrying toward town overtakes us with her flock of "cotton deer"—muzzled to discourage loitering. Stepping aside, we admire a newly mudded *na* and trace its owners' swirling handprints where this salve was smoothed on chapped walls to heal the erosion of the last rainy season. Traditional Maya houses like this one are downright fossilized; they have not varied in more than three thousand years. Proof of this continuum is scarce, since homes left untended soon re-wed the earth. One well-known example, the Maya house motif carved in stone on a ninth-century façade at the ruins of Uxmal, pictures an early twin of today's ubiquitous Yucatecan *na*.

Sally and I came across more evidence in war-ravaged El Salvador when we explored ancient Joya de Cerén, whose houses of mud, sticks, and thatch were identical to these in Zinacantan. Rousing a Maya guard from his siesta, we were led down chiseled steps, across wooden planks, and back through the centuries to the time when, late one summer night in about A.D. 590, this Maya Pompeii was buried beneath a fast-moving cloud of thick volcanic ash. Fourteen hundred years later a bulldozer excavating for silos uncovered the petrified village, and with it the average Classic Maya family's way of daily life and lodging. After examining a furrowed field of stubby, ossified cobs, we learned that the crumpled houses nearby gave up such everyday secrets as razor-sharp obsidian blades stashed safely out of children's reach, colorful ceramic pots tucked into adobe nooks, dishes dried and put away, steam baths, digging sticks, parts of a painted book, and pestles poised to grind. These were not a people huddled in mud huts. They read and were surrounded by beautiful objects. Even the poorest of Cerén lived a better life than many of their present-day heirs. What interested us most, of course, was the house painted iron-oxide red, clearly that of a shaman in his office of immolation. We were just as fascinated by tales of a family found clustered around a few polychrome vessels, a lump of blood red hematite, and chips of green jade. In a last-ditch effort to quench volcanic fury, these Maya had offered their gods a final sacrifice of colors. We left Cerén that day loaded down by the guard with fresh cashew fruits as well as confirmation of design continuity and color's bold, unbroken brush stroke.

Barking mongrels announce our arrival in "downtown" Zinacantan. Suddenly, from out of nowhere, a runaway bull—frothing white foam and trailing a broken halter—charges into our path near the plaza. Before his desperate owner can lasso him, the angry beast rushes past with nostrils flaring and slobbers all over Sally, much to the amusement of onlookers. Three years earlier a less sensational entrance took us past an ensemble of bubblegum pink, purple, yellow, and green adobe houses painted the very same colors as local weavings. We spent an hour talking

Weaver's House
San Lorenzo Zinacantan,
Chiapas, Mexico

tints with the extended family. "We favor the colors of flowers, of geraniums," the women specified, adding, "We paint at the holy time, at change of year and *cargo*." At their request I took snapshots of the children. Upon our return to the States, we posted prints to a sketchy address—and kept our fingers crossed.

Sally and I easily spot these same pelargonium-painted houses glowing at the edge of town. Today only the women and children are at home. Since all the braid-beribboned mothers wear long black skirts, flower-embroidered blouses, and capes of vivid pink, orange, and fuchsia shot through with sparkly threads, it takes a moment to locate the face we remember best among those in the swept-earth courtyard. Marta sits in shadow, nursing a newborn. Kneeling on reed mats, the others are tethered to backstrap looms, one end looped about the waist, the other tied to a yolk yellow porch column. Fingers flash in rhythmic passes as colors inch their way toward binding the family to Zinacantan and the eternal cycle. Daughters—miniature versions of their mothers

Yellow Shutters, Zinacantan, Mexico

—sit weaving too. They will copy until age seven, master by twelve, and marry by sixteen. Toddlers, whose curiosity cannot quite overcome their fear, hide from us behind burlap sacks of corn.

No one recognizes us, but no matter. We are simply welcomed as first-time visitors. A matron breaks the ice with the old refrain, "Does corn grow in your valley?" We inquire after crops and the latest baby. "It is my ninth," young Marta reports; for all pregnancies count, even those that never reach term. "They come like rain," says Marta, consoling childless Sally with a touch on the shoulder. "Rain is sometimes late, but it always comes." Just then my eyes fix excitedly on the set of portraits we had mailed, smil-

ing out of a reddish gold frame nailed beside a door. With this clue it does not take long for the family to realize that we are returnees and the source of these treasures from so far away. Words explode in crisp chirps and whistles as we are shepherded indoors—a sign of trust.

In the filtered darkness a young girl—baby brother packaged safely on her hip—scurries to the open fire smoldering in the female realm to the left of the door. She moves a few flame-blackened terra-cotta pots, then stirs the embers with such vigor that our eyes soon stream with sooty tears. Since a Maya house has no chimney, smoke must find escape through thatch or open eaves. To assist its flight, our junior hostess dares throw open the set of tiny, painted shutters. Windows—simply glassless holes in thick mud walls—number few, if any; the Maya believe that, given half a chance, evil and illness will enter on winds, as evidenced in creaking doors, fluttering wings, and quivering shadows. In the male domain to the right, a crimson, cloth-covered altar table displays a small, green cross, three lighted candles, and a handful of wilting yellow dahlias. We tally the other meager holdings: a long, low turquoise bench; striped orange water jug; straw basket nesting dried red chilies; galvanized pails filled with corn and beans; three wooden beds piled with blankets; and the dejected blade of a hoe. This single space serves as bedroom, closet, kitchen, pantry, and parlor for a whole family, now seven with the new baby. There is no bathroom; the toilet is just an open area out back. Electricity has come to Zinacantan's homes, even if running water has not; but this household has nothing to plug in. No conspicuous consumption here. These Maya possess only what they use each day. Fear of envy guarantees shared poverty.

The smoke still too dense, we retreat to the open porch, where large ears of yellow corn are strung by their husks to dry. "These bear strong seed," Marta says. Censed and displayed, their consecrated kernels contain the spirit of the maize; and one day next spring, these will prove again that death is not victorious if sacred duties are fulfilled. Unlike the Hoosier farmers of my home state, where corn is just a business, the Maya raise a holy crop. Here corn is caressed, comforted, and never, ever spilled or wasted. Babies' umbilical cords are cut against maize ears, thus binding the Maya as blood allies of corn from the moment of birth.

With their men away making milpa, the women decide among themselves that I may photograph their houses. As I work, two boys volunteer to teach Sally and me the colors in Tzotzil Mayan. After mastering their words for the yellow columns and the green house cross, I ask about the violet door. "Purple, blackberry, blackberry," they sing in Spanish, because all Mayan languages hold only five words for

Black Corn, Totonicapán, Guatemala

colors, those of the sacred directions. Pointing to a makeshift corn husk brush coated in last year's dried pink paint, we ask for the formula. "Burn limestone rocks for two days, then crush," the boys proudly reply. Marta chimes in, "Yes, mix lime, water, a little sugar, and powdered pink color from the market, not too hot, not too cold, to make things new again."

House upkeep is as cyclical as planting. In Zinacantan, as in much of the Maya world, a flurry of mud-plastering and whitewashing or painting in late December confirms the age-old custom of symbolically killing and then regenerating to start anew. Today's midwinter custom corresponds to the season when the sacred *yaxché* blooms—

the time of the creation of the world. Such ritual once required that all buildings, tools, and ceremonial objects in use during the previous months be "put to death" at the old year's demise. Everything from plates and bowls to shawls, stools, and braziers was tossed onto rubbish heaps outside of town and replaced with new. Pyramids, temples, and palaces were reborn with new coats of color, and simple houses were repaired and whitewashed. To deal the deathblow, the slain year's hearth fires were extinguished and then relit, bringing the power and protection of the yellow sun back into every home.

The Maya of today paint with this same mission. Their renewal rituals are based on the belief that all creations of the gods are imbued with *ch'ulel,* or an inner soul. Humans—the gods' greatest creation—receive thirteen red souls, which circulate in the blood. The Maya also believe that even those divine works we would consider inanimate—such as salt, lightning, mountains, and lakes—have an innate spirit force too. In contrast, works of human hands—from altars and houses to guitars and weaving spindles—must have their souls invested. Initially such souls are endowed through elaborate dedication rites demanding cleansing, sacrifice, prayer, and color. Forever after these souls are sustained through paint's annual resuscitation. To the Maya it is logical that color breathes life. Pigments, after all, derive from the living: tree sap, flowers, and crushed insects as well as rocks, gemstones, and the very earth itself. Saturated with their own vital spark from these soul-filled sources, colors awaken all they touch. Enshrined within the common act of painting, then, are behavioral shards linking these Maya to those who built the majestic empire of colors millennia ago.

Diamond Shutters
San Martín Sacatepéquez, Quezaltenango, Guatemala

The Italians say a house is not just a house, it is a story. A Maya house is even more. It is a living entity. Nothing important in the Maya world is just made; it also must be born. Only when endowed with a soul can a home bid gods and ancestors to enter and assist those within. This crucial ensouling is no mere ribbon cutting. Securing permission from a new home owner for Sally and me to observe and photograph this ageless ritual meant weeks of persistent inquiries and delicate negotiations through an obliging if slightly shady-looking character named Pepe. At last we gained approval to join a family dedicating their new home in San Juan Chamula. This village is the ceremonial center for 120,000 Tzotzil Maya whose dwellings spill down hills and across hamlets just a few miles north of rival Zinacantan. Proud, feisty, and inflexible, Chamulas were among the last to submit to Zinacanteco-aided conquistadors. To this day they tolerate neither deviation from tradition nor any non-Maya residents within their borders.

Two live chickens, bread, candles, flowers, soda pop, incense, and rum: this is our shopping list for a soul. At 171 pesos, or about U.S. $30, it seems a small price to pay to witness such a rite, though we realize it is about a month's wages to a Maya. We are told to come on Tuesday, an auspicious day when the gods are certain to be home. Evil runs rampant on Wednesdays, and on Sundays, ironically, "the door is closed and Holy Father will not hear our prayers."

When we enter Chamula center on this market morning, the tremendous plaza is enveloped in wood smoke, the caterwaul of cassettes, and a surging sea of blue shawls as women shop and gossip. Pepe leads the way uphill to a weary, whitewashed adobe with jade green pillars and a small sign proclaiming *H'ilol,* or seer, for to see is to have the powers of insight and healing. This is the home of Xalik, or Salvador Lunes Collaso, a respected, fifty-something Maya healer who long ago stood in the presence of the First Ancestors in his dreams and vowed to use his gifts for life. His Mayan name is that of an ancient Tzotzil god whose identity has since merged with the Catholic's greatest healer, San Salvador—the "sainted savior" Jesus—from

whom he takes his Spanish name. Since a *curandero,* or healer, is required for house ensouling, Xalik finds himself in the peculiar position of running his own show. In preparation he has suffered the requisite days of physical and moral purity: no misdeeds, sex, or quarreling sully his virtue. We miscreants are allowed to witness this private rite, Pepe explains, only because Xalik has lived, served, and saved souls long enough under Chamula's sun to stockpile much "soul heat," thus reducing his risk from envy's fury.

The eminent doctor-priest-diviner greets us in unexpected jeans and plaid shirt and waves us through his yellow "office" with hands deeply plant-stained from the forest pharmacy. Towering cases of Pepsi—"the choice of a new generation"—line one wall. This elixir is as key to Maya ritual today as Chamula's ever-popular *posh,* a bootleg brown-sugar rum. Xalik himself built and then painted turquoise the room's only furnishings: a table serving as altar on the east wall and a few small chairs, one hung with our host's ceremonial straw hat, dangling long satin ribbons. Like the vibrant feathers on yesteryears' glorious headgear, these ersatz plumes use their potent colors to pile up precautions against evil and illness. Xalik's walls are papered with pictures from magazines and calendars. Crudely framed in a place of honor are a yellówed newspaper clipping and a fuzzy blowup of Xalik in a woolly white poncho, looking small and uneasy, corralled by a press of dark suits. "Do you know the bush?" he inquires. "The bush?" we parrot, confused. Squinting closely at the photograph, we realize that one of the dignitaries pictured is indeed The Bush—President George Bush. Pepe explains that Xalik was once flown north to join in a Smithsonian conference on traditional ways. While in Washington, this *curandero* treated our nation's leader for "cold stomach" in a low-profile house call conducted on the White House lawn. "I save The Bush," Xalik claims with pride, "and soon I cure The Pope." His world is clearly much wider than we had presumed.

We trail Bush's savior into the family's older residence, where damp sticks hiss around a huge, blackened pot that has surely known many a sacrificed chicken. A cheeping brood of future kettle candidates scratches the dirt floor. One of Xalik's many daughters kneels beside the hearth, grinding, grinding, grinding, while a pair of black eyes peek out from the shawl tied across her back. Moving on through the household's tiny plaza, we reach the nascent adobe dwelling, naked but for an emerald door. "Why green?" I ask. Xalik hesitates, loath to release trade secrets. "I am *h'ilol,*" comes his vague reply. Then he adds with a smile, "And because this paint was left over from making crosses."

Mischievous giggles fill the new interior, where four of Xalik's grandchildren romp. Tossing fresh pine needles gathered from the wilds, they carpet the dirt floor and each other with this fragrant green gift for Yahval Balamil, the Earth Lord. Safe only for storage since its completion several months ago, this vacant house would have remained barren until Chamula's next major religious festival again funneled celestial attention on the village; but our offer to furnish the sacraments has boosted the date forward. Now our donations—battalions of bottles and columns of wax—march in symmetrical rank along an elaborate, stepped green altar blazing color from the eastern floor. They are grouped in

Ensouling, San Juan Chamula, Mexico

varying numbers that act as keys: thirteen unlocks the heavens, nine the underworld, and a lone bottle of purified water admits new beginnings.

Anticipating many influential guests, Xalik also sets this banquet table with vases of spicy white chrysanthemums, Holy Family portraits, an arbor of tropical greenery, and a clay chalice filled with charcoal and clumps of *pom,* a sticky incense made from the bloodlike resin of the copal tree. A large, jade green cross rises from the very center.

Assuming the role of the sacred *yaxché,* this vivid intersection between worlds will soon provide ravenous deities with food, drink, and prayers in exchange for a soul. The cross is carved with simple flowers and dressed with fresh yellow blooms, because flowers denote the divine. Since sweet aromas whet the appetite, every ritual menu includes the perfume of flowers mingled with the ambrosial smoke of *pom.* White candles, firmly planted in drops of their own wax "blood," are served as piping hot "tortillas." Thick or thin, they go up in flames just like *pom*—proof they have been relished. For libation there is *posh,* the "blood" of sugar cane. Poured in place of the ancestors' *balché*—a fermented tree-bark cocktail—*posh* is also imbibed by mortals during ritual to assist their staggering toward the transcendental realm where gods reside.

To the altar's right, a beautifully carved, raw wood harp reclines, awaiting life through paint. Switching on a small boom box, Xalik apologizes that the musicians hired to entertain the holy visitors are too drunk to perform. His tape's scratchy strumming, plucking, and bowing engulf the room in the same hypnotic strains that accompany all Maya ceremony. Bending over a slight depression in the floor, Xalik slowly claws out a square hole in the dirt with a broken machete. Registering its two-handspan depth, we are relieved that it's the musicians who are on a toot. Stories abound of inebriated *curanderos* falling headfirst into sacrificial holes. "But it isn't in the center," I quarrel. Xalik insists it is, pointing out the receiving porch included in his calculation. Without this ceremonial overhang, he stresses, a house is fit only for cattle.

On cue, Pepe scrambles into the rafters to tie a

Curandero's Chair,
San Juan Chamula,
Chiapas, Mexico

Chalk House
Zunil, Quezaltenango, Guatemala

Pink Awning
San Cristóbal de las Casas, Chiapas, Mexico

Door with Speckled Hen
Chicua, El Quiché,
Guatemala

slender rope from the ridgepole. This is not the first time a cord has dangled like a hangman's noose directly over this spot, nor is the pit empty. Feathered victims were sacrificed and buried in this grave when the house was "tamed" during construction. Materials harvested from the woods might seem free for the taking, but nothing in the Maya world comes without cost. What man wins from nature he takes from the landlord who owns the earth. Like many landlords and all ancient gods, Earth Lord is both good and evil, worshiped and feared. He grudgingly tolerates the lease of quadrants of his soil, trees, grasses, limestone, and water. In exchange he demands that his tenant acknowledge the loans and balance the timeworn ledger through ritual on his behalf. If the "rented" home goes hungry, Earth Lord will surely bite with illness or disaster. But by feeding the house a broth made from sacrificed chickens laced with chilies and *posh*—trickled into corners and tossed by cupfuls onto framing—the feral is tamed and Earth Lord's greed assuaged.

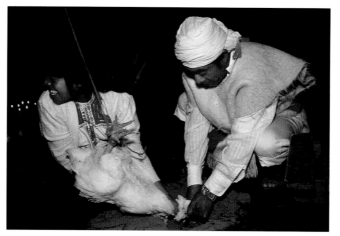

Sacrifice, San Juan Chamula, Mexico

Xalik vanishes while his nineteen-year-old daughter, Rosita, continues making ready. Her shy smile bares a Chamula beauty mark: glittering gold teeth. Pepe tells us that Rosita, too, has had the three dreams of a *curandera's* calling and now serves as Xalik's apprentice. Her father soon returns, resplendent in his dress whites: short trousers of bleached cotton; a fringed and felted white wool serape belted with a broad red sash; and a snowy, red-tasseled head scarf. On his left wrist he flaunts a bracelet of silver and turquoise, defying envy as he draws strength from its colored stone. The whole family now gathered and stilled, Xalik dramatically swings shut the mortal door and then opens the divine one by activating the altar with fire. First he lights the candles to burn brightly like "little yellow suns" and blind the eye of evil in this darkened void. Then he ignites the goblet of spicy *pom,* which Maya believe to be "the blue-green scent of heaven's heart."

His chanting is soft like a faraway song in a low, breathless timbre. There is no need to raise the volume; his gods and ancestors are close at hand. Palms cupping his eyes and feet tucked into a crouch, Xalik bows obeisance to the altar and the East. Dropping to kneel upon a tuft of black wool, he speaks to the earth, crosses and recrosses himself at head, heart, and lips, and then humbly presses his forehead into the soft pine shag. He rises. Waving the billowing censer, he speeds its pungent smoke swirling upward with his prayers, wooing the spirits of lightning, mountains, and lakes while summoning otherworld entities to feast. From time to time Xalik pours himself a shot of *posh* and always spills another on the needles, where it quickly soaks into the hard-packed floor. Earth Lord must be thirsty. But Xalik is not serving only gods; the house itself hungers for atonement.

Enter one plump white chicken. This bird—surrogate for the human blood let in ancient rites—has been penned up all week in chaste readiness and now struggles for freedom from Rosita's grip. If corn is the foundation of Maya belief, blood is the mortar. And blood is best spilled at high noon, that powerful yellow hour when the sun's heat is closest to this house. Firmly clasping the handsome rooster, Xalik binds its legs to the ominous rope, thankfully excusing us from witnessing the inspiration for the expression "running around like a chicken with its head cut off."

Posh forced down its throat in further consecration, this squawking trumpeter of dawn puts up a great flapping protest. Borrowing Pepe's pocketknife, Xalik positions Rosita's hands around the bird's head and feet, then plunges in the blade, slicing its throat in a neat, practiced motion. The bird's head drops into the pit. Wings keep beating the air and white feathers fly as nourishing red blood spurts into the underworld cleft. Averting her eyes at the fatal moment, Rosita reddens with shame. If she is to follow in her father's footsteps, she must soon steel herself to this sight. Downplaying the decapitation, Xalik nonchalantly wipes the blade on a scrap of paper. But this scalpel has severed more than a neck; the new home's umbilical cord has also been cut. This is the moment of birth. After less than an hour's labor, the "midwife's" own house has its soul.

As Sally and I had learned from Bonampak's murals, ensouling could entail much more elaborate ritual. In Classic times some dedication pits received rare, colorful gifts from the sea. Exquisite shells and corals, soft sponges, spiny urchins, and even briny living creatures were hauled far inland with much effort. These precious oceanic oblations supplied "pabulum" for a newborn soul, just as the great primordial waters nursed the first *yaxché.* When splattered with soul-suffused human blood and red pigment, the array of offerings was eternally united with the otherworlds. Although today's rooster is obviously more barnyard than marine, and his deftly buried head, feet, and feathers more fowl than fish, the bird's red blood, doused with three shots of *posh,* ensures that this Chamula cache also re-creates Creation as it heralds a new dawn.

Like ancient Maya priests, a tipsy Xalik has attained through *pom, posh,* and the beheading a sacred state where he can truly "see." As best he can, this *h'ilol* trims the candle wicks to slow their burning. Now that the gods have had their fill, they will listen; so prayers begin in earnest. Xalik sways to the four directions with reverent nods. Ringed in smoke and incantations, he orbits the room, his proffered censer wafting crosses before him. He concen-trates on each vital corner; for it is there, where old-style house posts extend deeply into the underworld, that evil can most easily enter. Sally and I are grateful when the droning cassette player gives up the ghost with one final, wobbling wail. At last we can recognize some words: Totil, San Juan, Htolik, Jesús Cristo, the five Maya colors—and I swear he throws in "tacos" and "Washington" for good measure. Part Catholic and part Maya ritual, Xalik's entreaties cover all the bases, with the color diamond's sacred directions invoked for their powers by this eloquent orator of hues.

Xalik prays in his Mayan tongue so the Old Ones will understand. Since Tzotzil "doesn't enter our ears," we rely on Pepe. "Four corners of sky, four corners of earth," "blue-green heart," "holy wood, holy mud, holy home," and "deliver from evil and envy," he interprets for us in whispered shorthand, admitting that this liturgy is an uttered scrawl that he can barely follow. According to Pepe, the endlessly repeated phrases boil down to, "Please take all that I can offer in exchange for what little I need. You are great, and I am insignificant." But whether kowtows or kudos, apologies or appeals, these words are mainly monologues to the Old Ones, or First Ancestors, the first Maya to plant corn, build houses, and praise the creators. Today their spirits reside in nearby mountains where they keep watch over the community. From this intimate vantage these model Maya punish those who stray from the well-trod path of custom and reward the steadfast.

The closed room strangles, and Sally squirms on the hard bench. Ducking to photograph beneath the cloud of dense blue blessings, I wonder if otherworld guests have sucked all the oxygen from the room or if it is just the syrupy *pom* coating my lungs. As a skyrocket whooshes off from the courtyard in thunderous salute to another notch in the petitions, a faltering Xalik commences yet one more circuit, the ninth. His billowing smoke forms a protective shield, fumigating every bump and shadow. Then unexpectedly, slipping two white blossoms from the altar, he

Red Door
San Cristóbal Totonicapán, Guatemala

Casa de los Piñateros
Hidalgo, Tabasco, Mexico

affectionately extinguishes the stubs of nibbled wax. The bargain is struck. With all the goings-on, we hardly noticed that Xalik's wife had whisked off the rooster's carcass to the old house for stewing. Now it returns in a pot; like any newborn, the fledgling house must be fed. Chicken soup soon stains the four corners, and we all eat what remains. It's one tough bird. Observing ritual etiquette, Xalik offers the first aperitif of *posh* to the unseen callers seated at the table's east end. Only then may we partake of the inaugural supper: chicken and chilies, downed with a bit of salt and corn tortillas, topped off by wheat rolls and coffee.

Xalik declares that the infant house is now "fragile, like a sick one." He prescribes that it be kept swaddled—shut tight for three days' rest—until a new sun is lit in its hearth and the family's souls have settled in around the rooster's bloody grave. This pit will be unsealed again if inhabitants are beset by sickness, bickering, or torment of fire—sure signs of a neglected house bawling for its regular feedings. Our healer would then intercede, warming up a spiritual formula of bread, rum, chocolate, tortillas, and a live black rooster, all to be buried to soothe the house's soul. But for now, contentment reigns. Xalik tells us of last Thursday's pickup truck ensouling while

Piñatas, Hidalgo, Mexico

the whole family downs fiery *posh* in equal shares. To drink is to play a part and sharpen vision; judging from its progressive effects, however, we are glad we secured a teetotaler's exemption for the sake of our own seeing. Yet somehow we feel intoxicated too.

The altar Xalik has opened will watch over both dwelling and occupants for the life of the house. Long ago, a Maya home was shelter-chapel-graveyard all in one, with its altar the focus of most rites and its packed-earth floor a shroud for the family dead. The Spanish successfully prodded much Maya worship into Catholic churches and moved Maya bones into consecrated cemetery ground. The home altar survives, however, as a focal point for daily ritual—guiding and cheering on its charges. Before this vigilant otherworld portal, everyday favors are negotiated with deities. Birth, death, and all life between take place within the holy table's view. The most basic home altar demands only a flat, four-cornered shelf, rude cross, and softly flickering candle to jump worlds. But when color and creativity are laid at its threshold to glorify the gods, envy need not be feared. Here, in cherished, Technicolor jumble, anything goes. Painted images of saints hobnob with fading family portraits. Plaster frogs and plastic dolls elbow first fruits of harvest and peacock feathers. Once we even saw a blue-tinted perfume bottle filled with holy water cozying up to a color TV, which also pulled in voices from another world.

Sally and I discovered our favorite home altar in swampy Tabasco State. Ancient homeland of the Chontal Maya, *tabasco* means "moist land," and indeed it is. This lush, buggy Eden blazes luxuriant green all day and then glows a smoky green all night as burning gases from its rich fields of black gold cremate Maya customs in their oily flames. Where so many sombreros have been swapped for hard hats, Sally and I must dig deeper for colors' roots. One morning, after poking around the adobe pyramids of Comalcalco, we ventured in our rented VW bug through miles of cacao plantations percolating with the fragrance of fermenting beans. Stopping to examine the bizarre, chartreuse pods of future chocolate bars, we glimpsed a patch of raspberry color beckoning in the distance. We eventually traced this hue to a painted concrete block house strung with clusters of piñatas. It was home to a large family of *piñateros* who had crossed that hazy frontier from Maya to Mexican. With strips of cane, bits of wire, flour glue, old newspapers, and gaudy tissue, this industrious crew concocts more than a thousand ruffled fantasies a year. "We supply the whole village. Each season and every child needs piñatas," declared fifteen-year-old Freddie as he laced a piñata with gunpowder to incinerate someone's sins this Easter. Waiting to be snapped up for festivals, birthdays, and even weddings, these spiders, sputniks, devils, angels, and Mickey Mouses scream their colors across ceiling rafters and out onto the porch, where a tiny paper Madonna smiles down upon the enterprise.

With a goofy purple burro in tow, we aim for the main highway but are soon lost, snaking alongside a bloated river. When we check our bearings with a woman toting two woebegone armadillos by their tails, the trio looks

Painted Coconuts, San Lorenzo, Mexico

back in unison the way we've come. Persuaded by their accord, we backtrack and lose ourselves again. A bright red house with cerulean shutters stops us in our tracks. Hearing our brakes, a silver-haired Maya coconut farmer rises from the shady cradle of a hammock and exclaims, "Welcome to our *rancherito.* My name is Carmen." Cautioning us to sidestep coconut meats drying on his patio, he pulls us in out of the heat and introduces his large family—and their beautiful altar. Beneath a maze of dangling hammocks in a room bound by pumpkin-colored walls, two cabinets, thick with generations of jade green paint, dazzle from atop a blood red table that floats on a deep blue concrete sea.

Tacked and taped with images of saints who guard its blue-green cross, the altar claims much of the scant floor space—proof of priorities. Presented before it are three fresh coconuts buoyed by indigo waves and drenched with the same sanguine paint as the table.

"I paint to honor and adorn," Carmen explains. "My oldest son, Evaristo, rides the bus to Villahermosa to gather the paint. There they have all colors. Each year when corn is yellow and we bend the stalks, I renew the altar. It is then I paint and place ripe squash and my best ears of maize upon green banana leaves. The land gives us what we need, not a lot, but enough. Life is very hard, but it is endured with the apostles. Ours is a holy house. When we pray here, we face east to Jesus. His home is in Jerusalem, that's in the east." Heirloom altars like Carmen's have amassed great powers with appetites to match. He tells of a neighbor who also inherited a family altar. "For two harvests this man made no offerings. He showed no respect. His pig died, his arm broke, and then his hearing left. Oh, there was much affliction! That was the year of little rain. We farmers spoke to him of his obligations. Now he is faithful, and since then all is good." We turn to watch as his wife, Trinidad, ceremoniously scrubs two plastic cups, expertly machetes open a coconut with one glancing blow, and then suspends its thick milk and sweet pulp in murky well water. Accustomed to scorn for Maya ways, she apologizes for what she serves. So although piglets drink from the same bucket and this is a time of cholera, we cannot refuse her generosity. Taking big gulps of the refreshing nectar, we offer silent prayers for microbial defeat and place our trust, too, in their resplendent altar.

*Home Altar
San Lorenzo,
Tabasco, Mexico*

Pink Pig and Painted Walls
Tlacotalpan, Veracruz, Mexico

Following age-old trade routes of the Putun Maya, Sally and I often wander beyond Tabasco into neighboring Veracruz. Although the only Maya still residing here are the Huastecs in the north, we sense Maya influence throughout the state. Fording the flat, watery world of coastal bayous in the south, where the Olmec first mined the color diamond that the Maya later polished, we always linger in the painted village of Tlacotalpan. This islandlike jewel is stunningly set in a broad loop of the Papaloapan River. Ringed in flowering water hyacinths, tiny Tlacotalpan, or "Middle of the Earth," vividly recalls the story of Creation, when land first bloomed like water lilies from out of the primordial sea. Conquered by Aztecs and Spaniards in furious succession, this site eventually became home to a tropical mix of native survivors, Sevillan aristocracy, and former African slaves brought to work the sugarcane. Today's languid town of fishermen and rocking-chair makers has fewer people each year as her young leave to escape the creaking pace.

Pure Spanish colonial, with its thick walls, tiled roofs,

Madonna Wall, Tlacotalpan, Mexico

and rhythmic arcades Tlacotalpan would be Andalusia but for one twist. Here, in startling contrast to the town's pervasive calm, every arch, door, parapet, and column is emblazoned in flamboyant, hand-mixed colors. "Tlacotalpan has the most *tintas* in all of Mexico," residents proudly proclaim. "Our house paints are strong and spirited. They give our town life and elegance." Unlike traditional Maya with their symbolic color code, Tlacotalpeños paint for the glory of the hues, governed only by their hearts. By day the sun's warmth arouses the scent of the sea as well as the colors of hibiscus, morning glories, and polychrome walls. When the mica blue sky shifts to purple, whole families

drag their rockers onto porches; and soon Tlacotalpan glows as the pastels and primaries painted so lusciously within spill out upon the velvety dark to join those waiting outside: watermelon, strawberry, tangerine, plum, mango, lemon, and lime—the tempting colors of icy *aguas* on a summer's afternoon.

If Veracruz and Tabasco have too much water, in an irony of weather their eastern neighbor, the Yucatán Peninsula, has too little. Mile upon desiccated mile, this great limestone skillet sears the Maya states of Campeche, Yucatán, and Quintana Roo to a crisp tortilla flat. Only sacred pyramids, brittle scrub, and the hot stones of whitewashed hamlets dare lift their faces to the glaring heat and break the parched monotony. Like thirsty critters seeking water, identical villages plunk down near every subterranean pool. Each sacred *cenote,* or natural well, is nucleus for a hulking mission church and clanking corn mill. These front a barren plaza drained of shade but for the rare *yaxché* still lifting the sky heavenward. Beyond this center lies a scatter of oval, palm-capped huts whose mud and rubble walls are seldom painted to avoid envy's wrath.

For a month Sally and I have been crisscrossing the Yucatán beneath a hard sun and cobalt sky, searching for painted color within these interchangeable towns. When a bus drops us amid a choke of exhaust and the whir of cicadas in the village of Kantunil, or "Yellow Stone," our efforts are at last rewarded. Kantunil stands out among her whitewashed cousins; here golden sunlight is built right into walls. Warm ocher paint imitates the local yellow limestone as it echoes the nearby gilded cathedral of Izamal, site of both ancient and modern Maya pilgrimage. This luminous yellow bathes both towns in a spiritual flush that restates the power of the sun at its zenith in a region where its strength is hard to ignore. The midmorning heat has swept the streets of all but one Maya couple. The woman, wearing a flower-embroidered white cotton shift, strides alongside her straw-hatted husband. A plastic tank of pesticide strapped to his back and a long machete thrust through his belt like a sword, he walks a clunky bicycle. We match pace and ask about their painted village. Her response is poetry. "Our land is sad and faded, so our houses must be joyful and alive. We like the rich yellow, burning bright as candles in a field that is otherwise all dust and stone." Her mate nods agreement, adding, "Our house is old and crumbling. It is in need of the strength of iron bars. But I can only give it yellow paint to hold it up another year."

Not far from Kantunil, the paint-flecked stones of the ruins of Chichén Itzá stairstep their way skyward. Nearly eight centuries ago, an Itzá Maya lord snatched the bride of Izamal's governor, sparking a war that pushed the Itzá out the back door of their magnificent city and south into the rain forest of today's

Maya Na, Tixcacal Guardia, Mexico

Guatemalan Petén. Here they raised Tayasal, an island citadel in a jungle lake that still bears the Itzá name. New refugees eluding the conquistadors eventually bolstered the ranks of this sanctuary. Tayasal's isolation—and lack of precious anything but a few souls to save—left it in relative peace long after the rest of Mesoamerica was yoked. As the last ceremonial center of the Maya, renegade Tayasal was still chanting rituals from illuminated texts and painting pyramids on which idols gulped human blood when

Harvard graduated its first theologians and lawyers not so very far to the north. Then in 1697 a Catholic priest, frustrated by Tayasal's resistance to his faith, steeped himself in Maya lore and wielded glyphic prophecies to persuade the Petén pagans that it was futile to resist the imminent death of their era. Accepting their destiny, the Maya swam ashore and disappeared into the jungle. As Spanish soldiers smashed the island stronghold to smithereens, the curtain fell on the last act of the conquest. Atop the rubble of Tayasal's temples rose the town of Flores. Today this tiny backwater is administrative capital of the vast, nearly empty Petén; but for Sally and me Flores is more a capital of colors.

Eager to examine this die-hard isle, we abandon our fruitless survey of Belize, where a melting pot of cultures means modern Maya are more visible in profiles than in paint. Crossing the border into Guatemala brings no change to the sweltering lowlands; but suddenly color courses as Maya blood thickens. Spurring our Honda down the sole road bucking west into the green Petén, we take paint's pulse in one malarial outpost after another. The landscape throbs with the fever-bright reds, blues, yellows, and greens that coat wooden-crate houses made of wide, horizontal planks. Their brilliant colors are barely dimmed by a powdering of dust that boils off the gravel strand to which they fasten like fluorescent pop beads. Garish, glinting huts of sheet metal flash past our windows. The material of their walls was meant to tin not Maya homes but the Jimex juice, ChocoMilk, or Texaco oil products whose logos are stamped across their façades in futile advertisement. And then we pass through time-warped "Calendarville," where every outdated porch is boldly papered in the cuddly puppies,

Boy and Golden Wall
Kantunil, Yucatán, Mexico

House of Painted Planks
Soslagunas, El Petén, Guatemala

Shutter and Hammock
La Venta del Sur, Choluteca, Honduras

Lagoon House
Flores, El Petén, Guatemala

Japanese pagodas, or Aztec "cheesecake" of an alien *cargo* that bounced off a passing truck some years ago. Twice we pay up at our favorite tollbooths, those imaginary blockades where hopeful Maya children have pulled a string across the lonely road to collect for right of passage.

Frazzled by the jarring drive, we surrender in Santa Elena, the noxious market sprawl oozing lakeside right before the Flores causeway. Breathing in shallow gasps of burning trash and diesel fumes, we take heart from our experience that just beyond the worst hellhole often lies a painted prize. Forgoing rowdy bars with exotic names and sleazy hotels with none, we circumvent a fetid rivulet of bilious swill, dodge piles of rotting papayas, and park the car. Ducking into a *farmacia* in search of a hit of hygiene and a prescription for local dining, we sidle up to the chest-high counter, where a ratlike dog pirouettes among the aspirin, combs, and open jar of sterilized cotton balls. Before we can voice our culinary question to the oily clerk clipping his nails, the repugnant *perrito* hops to the floor and mistakes my leg for a hydrant. We flee to Flores.

The next morning, revived by this islet's lively hues, Sally and I look up at a confectioner's palette of colors on some two hundred aging stucco petits fours.

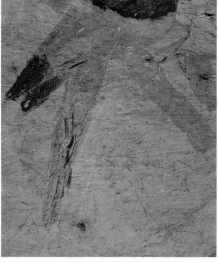

Earthen Parrot, La Campa, Honduras

In the dry season these houses are iced with intense pigments, but their colors quickly soften to glazes beneath the tropical sun and rain. Vivid brush strokes linger only where protected by arches of windows and doors. The lake is rising a little more each year; now its waters lap the crumbling walls, making sugary colors dance with reflected light while tin and tile roofs cast postage-stamp shadows. Climbing to the twin-domed church, we find no trace of the dozens of bloodied pyramids and thousands of painted idols

that once crowned the island. Spain's erasure was thorough. Since most tourists seek hard evidence of Classic times, they pass up this little town and head straight for the dramatic if denuded ruins of nearby Tikal. But Sally and I find the ancient Maya animated even more by walking upon Tayasal's stones while savoring this *pastelería* of painted walls.

Holding world title to banana republic, Honduras is among the poorest but most peaceful members of Central America's disorderly household. Putun Maya once sailed forth from her shores in great painted trading canoes. Today the country's few remaining Maya— most too poor to buy paint—cling closely to the baroque ruins of Classic Copán on the Guatemalan border. Due to poverty, much of rural Honduran color reverts to the genesis of painted decoration: colored muds from mineral-rich soils. Early one morning in a hardscrabble mountain village in the west, we watched a Maya housewife pat khaki walls as smooth as ironed sheets. Mixing water with earths the colors of mulberry, olive, cinnamon, and burnt rose, she swirled skilled fingers to populate her home with zinnias, parrots, hearts, serpents, and a long-tailed yellow cat. She framed it all in a cross-and-diamond motif borrowed from her beloved church and ancestors. As final gesture she signed her subtle masterwork with oxblood-colored handprints near the door.

One muggy afternoon along the lonely coastal highway of Honduras, a blue-and-green adobe house appears, flourishing a flaming red pyramid as big as its door. We rub our eyes in disbelief. Out front, a patient woman sits peddling five mangoes from a woven basket. Seated next to her, a young girl rocks back and forth. We ask the mother,

Red Pyramid
Ilamapa, Atlántida, Honduras

whose features speak of Maya lineage, how business goes; and then we broach the colors. "There is no reason," she insists. "All our neighbors like our house, but few paint. Many trucks pass, but no one has stopped before. My husband works in the cane fields. He painted it himself." Right then, up he strolls, two fingers missing from one hand due to a job liability like that of midwestern farmers. Appreciating our enthusiasm for his artistry, he reveals, "Coca-Cola asked to paint our home red and white, but we refused, despite the money they offered. You see, our youngest, she was born with twisted legs. She cannot walk. You see, her mind is weak, but she likes the colors. This is for my daughter. It thanks those who gave her to us." His words bear his tears. Like distant ancestors, he paints his pyramid. His blood offering. His prayer. As we pull away, yellow butterflies warming themselves on the pavement lift at our approach and shower down like confetti in the wistful breeze. That night we eat five mangoes, the sweetest we have ever tasted.

El 'Noa-Noa,' Retalhuleu, Guatemala

3
PAINTED CHURCHES
SINCE BEFORE THE MOON APPEARED

"It is a miracle from God!" exclaims the Maya cowhand, and I cannot agree more. Perhaps all the time Sally and I have been spending here in Tabasco's painted churches is paying off. Just a few hours ago we were hopelessly lost somewhere in the swamps along an unmarked, unpaved road as both temperature and humidity neared one hundred. It seems our halting Yucatec—*"¿Tush y am bé?"* (Is this the way to?)—had fallen short among the local Chontal Mayan speakers. After we stopped our car to study why landmarks did not match our map, the clutch refused to engage. Just then, the only vehicle we had seen all morning—a pickup carrying three men, a wilting cow, and two saddles—materialized out of nowhere. Incredibly,

Temple of the Feathered Serpent, Chichén Itzá, Yucatán, Mexico

OPPOSITE
Chamula Chapel, La Quinta, Chiapas, Mexico

the driver not only spoke Spanish but also knew a mechanic in the capital who would come and help. I hopped in back with the beef while Sally anxiously awaited my return. One delivered heifer, two repaired saddles, three Coca-Cola stops, and some four hours later, the car is fixed and we're back on the main road with our new friends leading the way. Now aware of our interests, the driver—with a honk and a wave—points out the turnoff for a little-known cluster of villages whose chapels he calls *"precioso."* The next morning, more confident of our directions, we set off to explore. Not far down the recommended road, a dazzlingly painted church appears, the first in a string of five—each no wider than the wingspan of an angel.

Painting God's house incurs no envy, since ecclesiastical color pleases the saints and thus enriches the whole village. From the flamboyant pilgrimage center of Cupilco to the polychrome chapels of Ayapa and San Isidro, Maya church painting reaches its pinnacle in Tabasco State. This spring Guaytalpa's is the standout, the gem of this poor village hidden in the marshes. Careful to avoid the peanuts and reeds drying in front of the simple adobe houses, we drive up to the plaza, where a crowd of small boys flying homemade kites parts before us like the Red Sea. Aside from the hammock seller drowsing on a bench in the gazebo, we see no one; but we can feel curious eyes watching from darkened doorways, a sure sign that strangers are rare. The façade of Guaytalpa's "sacred center" reads like an ancient lexicon: azure blue walls for vital rain, verdant green columns for sprouting corn, and blood red trim to ensure the sun's rebirth. These life-affirming hues loudly proclaim this chapel as pulsing heart of Guaytalpa and artery to the divine. So even though the village has no telephone, the colors confirm that here, the

Jeweled Christ, San Isidro, Mexico

most important lines of communication are always open. *"¡Qué hermosa!"* (How beautiful!) I say aloud. *"Sí, es brillante,* like a diamond," pipes up nine-year-old Jaime. His friends shuffle, giggling at his daring. We ask about the tiny silver charm hanging from a string around his neck. "It is a book," he whispers. "My mother tied it here so I will learn to read, with help from the *santos* who live in our blue temple."

Just as *pom* is the scent of heaven's heart, blue-green is its hue. To the Maya, every shade of blue and green is simply one word: *yax.* The color of the sky, water, jade, growing maize, and the *yaxché* planted at the center of the world, *yax* designates all that is precious and sacred. Sally and I will always remember the old Maya fisherman who first taught us this word while he painted his boat cobalt blue on a Yucatán beach. Motioning to a flight of green parrots glinting like emeralds across the burning sky, he declared, *"Yax, k'ul* [very holy]. The green birds, they are a blessing."

The blue-green of jade is also revered in Asia, probable birthplace of the Maya belief in a colorful, four-cornered world. In ancient times blue-green was the badge of Maya priests, royalty, and offerings to the gods. Sacrificial victims were sanctified with blue pitch, as were the temple steps they mounted and the stone on which they were flayed. During the midwinter Maya month of Yax, all objects of value—from spindle whorls and fishing nets to hunting darts and entry doors—were anointed with blue-green paint. These Maya knew that assistance from the other-worlds could be accessed anytime and anyplace through ritual and *yax.* In painting their great pyramids, however, they applied blue and green sparingly because these pigments were rare. But as the time of the Spanish drew near,

Painted Cornice
San Isidro, Tabasco, Mexico

Templo Evangélico
San Juan Ixcoy,
Huehuetenango, Guatemala

Three Green Pillars
Guaytalpa, Tabasco,
Mexico

prophecies and omens left the Maya little hope. Only then, in desperation, did beleaguered cities like Tulum and Mayapan secure enough blue pigment to coat their walls with its rejuvenating power.

Pyramids were usually drenched in red, a readily available pigment and itself a potent symbol of renewal. When the Spanish arrived, they banned red from religious architecture. To them this fiery color signified sin, the devil, and the human blood that they had seen smeared on far too many idols. In their attempt to blot out paganism, the Spaniards white-washed both temple-pyramids and the churches that soon followed. Inadvertently, the Catholic color of purity signaled to Maya the white of change. As the Maya gradually took on the upkeep of churches, they found their palette severely limited beyond plain white. With red prohibited, blue still prohibitive, and the black of death shunned, only one sacred color remained. The Spanish did not object to yellow, since it reminded them of their beloved gold. Today, however, with affordable, synthetic pigments and more autonomy, Maya—like these in Guaytalpa—can again call on blue-green and red to strengthen the bond with their pre-Columbian past.

Still carrying their colorful kites, the braver children push open wide the heavy church door and pull us inside to show off the humble *santos* as well as some wasps furiously molding a mud abode beneath a niche. Guaytalpa's chapel, like most in the Maya world, is rarely locked or empty. Today a dozen worshipers linger within this cool, dark, blue-green sanctuary strung with red and yellow crepe paper streamers. En route from the mill, women kneel to pray beside their plastic buckets of ground corn, savoring a moment's peace and luxury before returning to the heat and dirt floors of their homes. Men come

Conquest, Panchimalco, El Salvador

straight from the fields with their machetes, each stopping before San Isidro's chartreuse altar, where a pair of quail eggs and a double ear of corn have been left as payment to this patron of farmers. Across the room a red guitar leans in the corner near a striking, long-faced Virgin in black pleats and embroidered shawl. She cries for her bruised and bloodied Son, who is stationed in the next alcove. Head in His hands, this dark-skinned Christ wears an apron of blue sequins and a wincing brow. The sacristy behind the main altar is a dusty tangle of everything from the ephemeral to the everlasting: electric cords, processional masks, tattered paper lanterns, tarnished urns, charred arch-angels, stacks of turquoise chairs, and fireworks for the approaching Easter fiesta. On one wall, just below the nest of a cooing dove, a child's crayon drawing of a stepped pyramid, taped beside a framed photograph of the smiling pope, reminds us that Maya conversion to Catholicism is anything but complete.

When Spanish missionaries first reached the Maya lands, they hoped to reinforce Christian supremacy by ripping down temple-pyramids and using the tumbled stones to erect consecrated houses for their own "true" God. However, by raising new churches upon the foundations of Maya ruins, the Catholics unwittingly built a visual and emotional bridge to the Maya past. The priests fared no better with their crosses, which the Maya immediately recognized, painted blue-green, and worshiped as sacred *yaxché* just outside the new "temples." To finance their ambitious building projects, the missionaries exploited Maya colors. Profits from natural colorants—the blue of indigo from El Salvador, reds and blues from Belize logwood, crimson cochineal from Guate-mala, and purple from sea snails along the Chiapas coast— were second only to Mexican gold and Honduran silver

Arc Walls
Xela, Quezaltenango, Guatemala

Corazón
Santa Margarita,
El Quiché, Guatemala

*Evangelical Flame
Chupol, Sololá,
Guatemala*

*Mask and Skyrockets
La Campa, Lempira,
Honduras*

until the mid-nineteenth century, when cheap aniline dyes destroyed this lucrative export market. The Maya were forced to labor for the dye industry as well as the new religion. Constructing churches in the style then fashionable in Spain, they readily embraced Baroque's sweeping, sensual ornament, which inspired worshipers to transcend earthly bounds—an itinerary already quite familiar to the Maya. But they did not copy impassively. Within Spanish patterns Maya craftsmen implanted traditional symbols, colors, and numbers: angels swaddled in blue-green plumes; a baptismal font carved with corn, birds, and stars; or thirteen steps to a jade green door studded with nine red florets. Spaniard and Maya could each read these as they pleased. Eventually the Maya recognized these churches as community assets to be faithfully tended and adorned.

While the transition from temple-pyramid to church was relatively smooth, the meeting of Old and New World beliefs was jarring. Once the Vatican finally determined that the Maya did indeed have souls, Europeans had to reconcile their faith with the existence of a heathen people and strange creatures never mentioned in the Bible like anteaters, iguanas, and jaguars. Meanwhile, bewildered Maya were told to stop worshiping their wooden idols and holy books and instead pray before the friars' wooden images and Holy Book. Yet the People of the Corn knew they must fulfill their crucial contract with the gods; for just as maize cannot reseed itself, Lord Sun cannot continue on his path without man's help. But how could an unknown god from another land care for the maize fields or understand the prayer for rain? This new god did not even speak Mayan. So when Spanish priests put the tourniquet on blood sacrifice, the Maya had to lead a double life in order to survive. They

Feeding San José
Chichicastenango, Guatemala

attended mass for their earthly masters and performed ancient rituals for their divine ones. Partners in collusion, the Spaniards transposed Catholic saints onto Maya gods—finding the closest match in attributes and feast days—at the same time as the Maya grafted their old gods and colors onto saints. Still today, Saint Michael often masks the red rain god, Chac; Saint James the Pilgrim stands in for the black merchant god; the blue Virgin Mary embodies the moon goddess; and resurrected Jesus updates the golden sun god, who is resurrected not just once but every morning. The Maya simply added to their pantheon, finding nothing contradictory in these holy hybrids.

The monumental task of even superficially Christianizing the Maya was eased by similarities between the two religions. Whether "diabolical parodies" or "God's wisdom in preparing the way," these overlaps were uncanny. Besides sacred statues and crosses, both Maya and Catholic independently relied on flowers, incense, and fire in ritual; placed their altars in the east; performed acts of confession, fasting, baptism, and communion; and revered kings who purchased salvation for their people with their own blood. But there were real differences as well. Catholic prayers focused on a heavenly afterlife, while Maya prayers concerned matters of this world, like health, fertility, and harvest. Catholics equated the earth with hell, while to the Maya, earth was the source of life and corn. And threatening hell was of no use; Maya knew the underworld was the destination of all souls, good or evil. Eventually awakening to the fact that their "uncorrupted children of God" had no interest in being saved, most early clerics gave up. This left the unshepherded Maya several centuries to fuse Catholicism and folk ritual into unorthodox amalgams that continue to this day. The Catholic Church has since tried to reclaim its flock and, more recently, to standardize belief. But most Maya villages—whether antagonistic toward any outside interference or just too small and isolated to warrant more than occasional words from a circuit padre—still maintain their own ways of worship, here in Guaytalpa and across the Maya world.

As I work, dragonflies float in and out of open shutters. The boys line up along one pew, thrilled when I call them over to view a *santo* through my lens. Fearing noise could affect the outcome, six-year-old Ernesto wags a finger to hush the room each time I am ready to shoot. When I finish, I hand him a ten-peso piece for all nine friends to share. Delighted, they dash across the plaza, where we join them as they buy six sodas and three candy bars. Jaime hands us back the single peso change. As the first cool shadows of dusk wash up the blue church walls, we ask the Maya shopkeeper about the colors. "Each December all Guaytalpa takes part in the painting," he replies. "I live beside the church, so I must paint, too. Not to do so would dishonor the saints who live next door. Ah well, we do not have so much corn. We each give what we can. Our gift is rich colors. We paint with our hearts." That evening, returning to the capital, we pass a Maya child

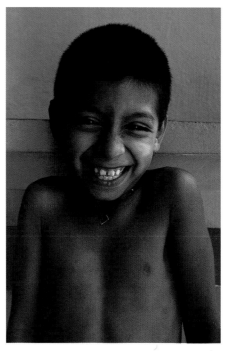

Jaime, Guaytalpa, Mexico

sitting beneath a street lamp alongside the highway. With pad and pencil in hand, he uses the state's electricity to finish his homework. We think of Jaime and his silver book.

To the ancient Maya, works of man, such as temple-pyramids, had a definite life span and then died. Maya themselves were said to have a life span of fifty-two years, as determined by their intricate system of measuring cyclical time using both their sacred and solar calendars. The Sacred Round was a ceremonial calendar of 260 days—divided into thirteen months of 20 days each—equaling both the period of human gestation and the growing cycle of highland corn. The Solar Year of 365 days divided time into eighteen months of 20 days each plus 5 lost days—the white days of change, when evil reigned while the sun was renewed. Every fifty-two years these calendars intersected in a powerful instant when one era died and another was born. The Maya also tracked linear time with their Long Count, which traced time back to the creation of earth and its colors, and projected time forward into infinity. Together, these three calendars were the framework upon which the Maya hung history, prophecy, and belief.

The life span of ancient buildings was based upon multiples of the Long Count's twenty-year units. Every 260 and 400 years whole cities were rebuilt to mark the beginnings of the most significant Long Count eras. Just like their makers, dead buildings required a releasing of their souls through elaborate burial, or "termination rituals." As long as a building was occupied, its powers were safe and grew stronger, but when its time had elapsed, a space could be used no more. Abandoned on death, its soul force became dangerous to the family or community unless the soul was "killed." The old structure would be brutally mutilated—stripped of its paint and stucco, slashed, smashed, broken, and burned. Key to this killing was the removal of all soul-suffused color, for color was life itself. After death, however, ancestral buildings—like ancestors—were not soon forgotten owing to the holiness they had acquired over their lifetime. Temples, the most important buildings, accumulated the greatest sanctity. Within painted temples high atop sacred red mountains, entranced Maya kings stood with arms outstretched, draped in blue-green quetzal feathers and jade.

Embroidery and Lace
San Andrés Xecul, Totonicapán, Guatemala

Niche with Orange
Santa María Tonantzintla, Puebla, Mexico

Mass
San Andrés Xecul, Totonicapán, Guatemala

Thus transformed into human *yaxché*, they bound the mortal world of their subjects to that of the gods through sacrifice of drops of their own blood together with the aromatic blood of the copal tree. With each new ritual performed, spiritual residue was left behind, and the membrane separating worlds became more permeable. And so it was upon such sacred spots that new temples would rise—each one more powerful, a little higher, and closer to the heavens than the last—with a new soul, new life, and new colors.

Temple-pyramids are thus time capsules encompassing layer upon layer of history and death. But in western Honduras, at the Maya ruins of Copán, Sally and I were privileged to study one Classic temple—discovered in 1989 and named Rosalila—that was an exception to the rule. This temple had been buried "alive." Our guide, Professor Oscar Cruz—chief conservationist here for twenty years—unlocked a small, wooden door in the side of Copán's tallest pyramid, which stands at the center of the sacred Acropolis. We entered onto a dark, narrow warren whose shored-up walls of hardened mud and stone were barely lit by a string of naked bulbs. Cruz then led us across scaffolding and catwalks, deep into the pyramid's bowels. The sub-terranean air was damp and close, the tunnel disorienting. When our eyes adjusted to the darkness, we found ourselves facing a small temple hidden at the ancient city's very heart.

San Sebastián Mártir, Gracias, Honduras

"Rosalila is unique," said the professor. "It was never defaced, never terminated. Great effort was expended not to damage it in any way. Some fourteen hundred years ago it was awarded reverential burial above other, even older temples, after its brightly painted stucco was carefully wrapped in a thick coat of plaster. See here the pristine masks, the gods, the colors. The temple's soul is still intact.

But why, this is our mystery." We looked across the temple's face at delicate details of molded deities still flecked with rich reds, yellows, and greens. "Rosalila is a holy mountain, a sacred mountain," Cruz repeated excitedly as we struggled to keep pace with his rapid Spanish and motionings. "Deep beneath this floor lie the sacred waters of the underworld. And the roof comb holds the sky god, the great celestial bird with its huge, blue-green wings. See here, it rests atop the branches of the sacred ceiba, crowning the Maya universe."

As we stepped through a stone portal, Cruz continued. "Right where we now stand is the center, Centro Rosalila. Here, behind this wall, inside a red room, we found an offering to commemorate the temple's burial: a stone jaguar incense burner, jade beads, oyster shells, stingray spines, and nine mystical, chipped flints. These were wrapped in blue-green cloth, and all were covered in great quantities of powdered pigments of red and green. We now believe that Rosalila was not ritually killed like all the other temples because it may entomb the founder of Copán's lineage, Yax K'uk Mo', or Blue-Green Quetzal Macaw. A powerful *curandero*, he was also known as First Tree, for he was Copán's seed. Such a tree would never be uprooted. His tomb may lie deep beneath our feet. We are looking for it now." As Cruz relocked the door on the pyramid's mysteries, he added, "This place can never be opened to the public. Its colors are too fragile and its solutions to Maya riddles too precious to risk."

Sally and I see them from a distance, walking beside the road. The man wears a tattered brown jacket; his wife, colorful woven stripes. Both are bent nearly double beneath stacks of firewood. They must have been gathering branches all morning in some forest of this mountainous province of El Quiché, whose name, like Guatemala's, means "Many Trees." When our rented pickup truck pulls alongside the pair, their eyes lift to meet ours. Straining faces turn to smiles as they offer up soft-spoken *buenas* for "good afternoon" and accept a ride. Helping them load their wood, we notice that the man is missing one arm. "The war," he explains, referring to the bloody "civil conflict" that has raged here for decades, killing countless thousand Maya, forcing another million from their milpas, and continuing the chain of suffering and violence first set in motion by the conquistadors. Since the couple is bound for San Sebastián Lemoa, now so are we. From translations of the ancient Popol Vuh—the remarkable Quiché Maya book of creation that speaks of hero gods and holy places—we know that five sacred lakes mark the quadrants and center of this realm. At its blue-green heart lies Lemoa, or "Mirror Waters." The holy water of this tiny lake, collected by shamans from all over the highlands to assist with divination and curing, contains the wisdom and power of the four directions and their colors. Just as we sight a rather ordinary-looking pond, we hear tapping on the back window. We stop and help our passengers unload, refusing their payment. "May God repay!" they wish us before disappearing into a pinewood.

Across the road a woman fills a plastic jug at Lemoa's well. Balancing the burden atop her head, she begins the steep climb to the plaza. We follow as far as the timeworn, whitewashed church, which buried ancient temples attuned to much older prayers. At the foot of its stairs, amid corn husk wrappers of *pom* and the sludge of clotted wax, a sooty shrine puffs wisps of sweet smoke heavenward. Ascending the stone steps, we enter a blue-washed room where two

Painted Niche, La Jigua, Honduras

men are busy painting. Another man changes a lightbulb over the head of a gaunt San Juan while a woman arranges blue irises in a powdered-milk tin at the saint's feet. It is the time of tuberoses, and their heady fragrance fills the sanctuary along with the muted notes of a rural accordion and violin drifting in from a back room. We are greeted by a bright-eyed church guardian with a shock of gray hair, who holds an iron ring of keys in callused hands as rough as sandpaper. He tells us that Lemoa is preparing for the festival of their patron, San Sebastián, and then introduces this arrow-pierced saint, whose wounds have just been freshened with red paint. "Here we are very Catholic, very Christian," he declares. "Soon the priest comes, and we have mass and baptisms." We ask him about this room, now half-blue, which will soon be white. "Long ago these walls were yellow, for this is a holy place of corn," he chronicles. "After this they were made the color of our lake. But blue grows dark with smoke, so now we make it the color of clear light. The altars, they are always red. It is our custom. Red is the color that keeps the *santos* happy."

The contented *santos* that he speaks of form a family of some two dozen richly painted living gods who reside here within glass-faced cabinets of papaya green, coral, aquamarine, and crimson. An ecstatic jungle of leaves, vines, zigzags, and curlicues embellish these cases, many haloed with red wooden sun rays. The glass door on San Antonio's yellow home is smeared with kisses and a waxy cross drawn with votive drippings. Loved and respected, each saint is a confidant, as easy to talk with as neighbors; for all are Maya, even those whose features or clothes look Spanish. Most bear small, round mirrors, each a tiny model of Lemoa's reflective lake and just as capable a gateway to the otherworlds. "The *santos* are the caretakers of our village," explains the guardian, fondly nodding to the rough carvings. "They watch over us day and night. Have you saints to watch over your land? Does San Sebastián have a brother there?" Sally assures him that his patron has many relatives in El Norte, though our saints are not as old. "It is my *cargo,* my charge, to keep this church," he continues. "I serve the *santos'* needs. Each day I speak the names of the holy ones and feed them with prayers, incense, flowers, and candles. We are put on this earth to praise God and the saints. We do not neglect them, and they do not desert us," he says, gesturing to this great banquet hall and its many tables laden with "food" for honored friends.

Marvelous legends abound—starring seductive brooks, talking iguanas, and enchanted trees—to explain the arrival of *santos.* Early priests could hardly deny such tales, since holy images were popping out of hiding places all over Spain after the fifteenth-century expulsion of the Moors. But when Sally asks the origins of Lemoa's saints, "Divine hand" is the only reply. Today, as with Maya idols of long ago, sacred images carved from the wood of *kuché,* or cedar, the "god tree," are the most esteemed. But no matter their source or substance, Maya saints are living beings. As such, they desire regular baths, daily news, and warm, clean clothes. And just like people, some are kind; some, ill-tempered. All but the agoraphobes get bored by the monotony of life on a shelf, longing to wander or line up near the church door to listen to a marimba or watch a feast-day dance. Some images conduct love affairs. Even a Virgin Mary must sometimes be separated from certain *santos* during processions to ensure she won't slip off with an old flame, fanning jealousies and church fires!

"The *santos* will scold me in my dreams if their home is dirty or its paint is chipped," says the guardian. "Then they might throw stones down upon me from the walls. Sometimes we must show them what our village needs as well. Sometimes we take Older Brother Christ and San Miguel up the hill to let them see our dry fields so they know to give rain." And if they don't, Sally and I have heard

that Maya may dress a *santo* in bright green, dunk him in the low river, lock him up, or even bury him as a reminder of lapsed duties. Before we leave I ask why the church façade is painted white. "I do not know," the old man admits. "This I did not witness, for this temple was here before I was born." And the age of his charge? He thinks carefully and then responds, "Ah, *sí, tiene años* [it has years]. It has been here since before the moon appeared."

Some years later, on our fourth visit to Lemoa, Sally and I spot a nun drawing water from the town well. We soon learn she is one of three American Maryknoll sisters—Lilla, Helen, and Rose Mary—now living in the cloister of Lemoa's church. After I spend the morning photographing *santos,* we sit with the nuns in their sunny garden and talk about their chosen austerity and rewarding work helping Lemoans rebuild their lives and faith. They tell us that their contemplative order was forced to retreat from El Quiché in the late 1970s after the murder of a dozen priests; they began returning in the mid-1980s, once the worst of the violence had subsided. During their absence, this convent where they pray today was used as a torture chamber by the army. When we describe our project, the sisters offer to accompany us to the cemetery just west of town. Along the way, a Maya mother stops to reverently clasp each sister's hand as we pass. The graveyard, as poor as the village, is just a small clearing with low earthen mounds, a few painted crosses, and three simple monuments. But Sister Lilla says that there is something very special here that we should see. She points to a stone marker inscribed with a diamondbacked snake and the words, "These tombs safekeep the twenty-six massacred martyrs buried in a clandestine cemetery in 1981–82 in San Jose Pacho, giving their lives for peace. Your blood fertilizes our land, brothers and friends. We will not permit impunity. No more clandestine cemeteries. Village of Lenoa [*sic*], 22 November 1992."

All over Guatemala the blood-soaked earth is beginning to speak of the tens of thousands of Maya who have been dumped into shallow, anonymous graves. Lemoa is

Red Table, Red Cross
San Sebastián Lemoa,
El Quiché, Guatemala

Souls and Skull
Caiquin, Lempira, Honduras

no exception. Sister Lilla relates, "The bones of the Lemoans buried here were discovered outside a nearby village. These husbands, sons, and brothers were identified by their wives, mothers, and sisters, who recognized their own tattered weavings among the remains." The sisters remind us that each piece of woven Maya cloth bears not only the unique pattern of a village but also the special "signature" of its maker within its subtle variations. In recent decades many Guatemalans have discarded traditional dress for *ladino* garb in order to conceal their origins and avoid drawing fire, especially when they hail from a region of guerrilla activity. Sister Lilla goes on to say, "Lemoans quickly built twenty-six pine coffins to carry these bodies the five hard miles to the cathedral in Santa Cruz del Quiché, where mass was said, and then another five back here for burial. The survivors were grateful to finally reunite with their missing. Villagers told us that the dead need to stop their wandering and rest. They need to be near their loved ones, just as the living need a place to speak with their dead. Now these names will not be lost, and the community can begin to recover its soul."

A few months later, when Sally and I are back in California, the sisters write of tragedy. Bandits have broken into Lemoa's church and stolen many of the precious *santos*. The villagers are stunned and brokenhearted. With their good friends and saintly guardians kidnapped, the Lemoans must feel vulnerable too. As requested, I quickly send photographs to assist in the search. These are shown to antiques dealers who might be approached by those hoping to profit from the growing international traffic in religious artifacts. The nuns' next update tells that a ring of thieves has been caught red-handed robbing a neighboring church. In the ensuing struggle, one of the culprits—a

Crosses, San Sebastián Lemoa, Guatemala

Lemoan—was killed by the enraged congregation, but there is still no trace of the *santos*. "The villagers pray to the darkened silhouettes in empty cabinets," the nuns confide, "all that remains of the cherished statues." Recalling the old guardian we had met there many years ago, we ask the sisters how Lemoans are dealing with their loss. "Villagers do not blame themselves," they write. "They do not consider this a personal judgment. They know other churches have also been robbed. The disappearance is seen as evil and offensive to God, but it is accepted, like so many other disappointments and sufferings in life. Yet the Lemoans survive and rejoice in their faith, displaying a trust far beyond our own." Sadly, villagers have had to resign themselves to the fact that the lost *santos* may never find their way home.

"Chiapas Poised for War" and "Zapatistas Threaten New Attacks," scream the headlines in San Cristóbal de las Casas. Doors slam and shutters bolt as residents and tourists alike scramble out of town. All anticipate trouble on New Year's Day, the first anniversary of the Maya rebels' brief takeover of this city. Here in Mexico's poorest state, where thunderous cascades generate vital electric current for much of the country, powerless Maya—long out of land and patience—generate high-tension political current. Chiapas now recognizes two opposing governors, one for the official state, the other for the "state of war." Mexican troops maintain a tight cordon. The bishop is on a hunger strike. A truce is called; its deadline expires. Only press and television crews roam San Cristóbal's oddly silent streets, where painted walls explode in angry scrawls: "The blood is on your hands, Mexico," "Assassin army out of Chiapas," and "January 1st lives."

Feeling increasingly isolated, Sally and I have been

*Hand of the Saint
Santiago Atitlán,
Sololá, Guatemala*

Village Santo
La Misión, Lempira,
Honduras

holed up here for weeks, reading in the Na Bolom Maya research library. Whenever cease-fires are declared or roadblocks lifted, we slip out to nearby Maya centers like San Juan Chamula and San Lorenzo Zinacantan or to more remote hamlets with ancient Mayan names like Kanalumtik, Natoc, and Kakumchich: Land of Stars, Home of the Clouds, and Burned Blood. Last week en route to Ocosingo, we waited several hours for an armored convoy of generals to pass. Yesterday a soldier peeked out of a tank's gun turret to snap our picture while I photographed in the Santo Tomás Oxchuc cemetery. And later that afternoon a Maya grandmother in San Miguel Huixtán, while painting over political graffiti sprayed across her house façade, told us, "Blue covers the age of my walls, for it is strong. We need its strength to heal the wounds of war."

On most of these excursions it is the rural churches that enchant us, but in these most conservative of Maya villages churches are off-limits to cameras under threat of confiscation or even stoning. Nevertheless, Sally and I persist in our attempts to gain permission to work inside the sanctuary of San Andrés Larrainzar. This seventeenth-century mission is a treasure trove of primitive, Maya-featured *santos*. Lining the walls of their cavernous yellow room, they mesmerize with their large, staring eyes, huge hands and heads, heavy mouths, and opalescent complexions. These divine benefactors are all strung with their riches: colorful necklaces of satin ribbons, antique coins, flashing mirrors, and red and yellow fruits. Some stand buried beneath layers of the local weaving, which replicates the diamond color cosmos in its wondrous brocaded patterns; others are lavishly gowned in painted, chiseled pleats. Those saints who suffered most during the decade-long

Festival Mass, Santa María de Jesús, Guatemala

Mexican Revolution of 1910 now huddle cracked and twisted near the entry door, barely rescued from the violence of those anticlerical times.

These saints are blood relations, the villagers say. And it was their beloved patron, San Andrés, who chose this site by a stream to build his own home. He had help from his younger brother, San Miguel, and their two sisters, Santa María Magdalena and Santa Marta, all of whom serve as patrons of nearby hamlets and visit every festival. As part of the effort to purge Mexico of Catholicism after the Revolution, the village was saddled with the name Larrainzar in honor of a *ladino* politician, but this did not dampen enthusiasm for the real founder. These Maya continue to call themselves the "children of Our Father San Andrés" and their village by his name. Like their Chamula neighbors, Andresanos remain aloof and independent. Armed with machetes, they chased most *ladinos* from their territory twenty years ago and then tried to expel Protestants and the Catholic priest. Since any departure from the norm is so unwelcome here, it is not surprising that no one is willing to risk offending his community by even discussing my request to photograph.

Today the roads are open again, and we arrive hopeful, armed with letters of commendation from consuls and clergy, a new friend, Celso, who speaks fluent Spanish, and the knowledge that Fiscal Diego—a church official who has eluded us for weeks—will surely be on hand. A group of young boys race ahead of us, remembering our earlier inquiries and yelling Diego's name. We find him sequestered in the sacristy, counting a plate of coins. When Sally leaves some pesos before a Virgen del Rosario, we finally get his attention; he advises that feelings will be hurt unless all the saints are fed equally. Sparkling at my offer to pay the *santos* in exchange for their portraits, Diego explains that I will first need community consent. For the next few hours the fiscal, Celso, and I march back and forth between the church and town hall. Trailing an ever-growing crowd of spectators, we search for an elder who can read my Spanish letters while we round up the *cargo* officials who will hear my appeal.

In San Andrés, as all across the Maya world, saints watch over the village, and *cargo* holders watch over the saints. The ancient version of the *cargo* system, which nourished the divine *yaxché* and kept the sun on course, was transformed into religious brotherhoods by early Spanish priests as a tool of conversion and control. Gradually these fraternities evolved into autonomous societies that continue to fulfill each community's ritual obligations. Like the old gods demanding blood offerings, today's saints also insist on great sacrifice. Religious *cargo* is costly, requiring a year's worth of candles, incense, soap, fresh flowers, and paint, all to keep

Ceremonial Hats, San Andrés Larrainzar, Mexico

saints smiling and well fed. The greatest expense of all, throwing the patron saint his annual party—with the festival food, drinks, fireworks, costumes, and marimba bands this entails—squanders a whole year's wealth in a few days' time to protect the village from the envy of gods and men. If a man refuses his share of this burden, he is reminded that *cargo* is a small price to pay for immunity from misfortune. So with help from wives, men spend much of their lives climbing the *cargo* ladder. Resting between rungs only to recover from debt, they serve in ever more demanding positions until they attain the elevated status of village elder and are then consulted on all important matters.

"Come and speak. We will listen and hear," proclaims a patriarch to open the proceedings. A host of civic and religious officials has finally assembled in this small, cold meeting room. Most of the crowd wear the uniform of their office: heavy black wool ponchos tied twice with red sashes. Their beribboned straw hats hang from hooks on the wall. As petitioners, Celso and I must stand while the Andresanos sit, with those of highest status closest to the east just like *santos* in the church. Women are excluded from this council, so Sally and Celso's wife, Ginny, wait outside. A dignitary holding a silver-headed staff from which dangle red ribbons like rays of the sun asks the mayor to present my request in Tzotzil. Signifying the import of this meeting, a holy band with harp, guitar, and two-stringed violin scratches out the eternal tune of the saints. My letters circulate around the room, their stamps, seals, and signatures scrupulously inspected.

A rambling debate ensues in which all have equal voice. Nothing is translated into Spanish other than occasional questions relayed through three languages. "How many photographs are desired?" "Exactly what pictures will you take?" "How will these be used, and why?" With Celso's help I try to explain my interest in their painted *santos*. I tell of the people in my country who study such things and would like to know about the saints who live in this village. I add that since these *santos* are so very old and powerful, my photographs could be a valuable record for the village and the world. I know these men do not speak for themselves but as proxies for the saints, so each of my answers is carefully weighed, eliciting candid approval or displeasure. Finally, I offer to deliver a copy of my book once it is published. "A book is of no use to our people, for

Baroque Column
Zunil, Quezaltenango,
Guatemala

we cannot read," comes a humble reply. In the end, consensus is reached: "Permission denied. No photographs allowed." I could plead my case no further. I wonder if I have tripped over current politics until a younger man tells Celso, "If a camera displeases even one saint, our whole village could be imperiled. We cannot accept your money. The images of our saints are not ours to sell."

From an inconspicuous perch between the twin bell towers atop Zunil's baroque church, Sally and I watch weekly market-day transactions unfold. The musical murmurs of Guatemalan tongues float up to us from the plaza's throng as highland Maya quietly barter: a skein of yellow twine for two brown eggs, conical cakes of salt for green onions, and balls of black soap for pink plastic shoes. Wrapped in ankle-length shawls of scarlet, fuchsia, and violet, Zunil women create a rich, undulating tapestry as they thread among pyramids of tangerines, radishes, chilies, and bananas, all displayed on squares of intensely colored cloth. Neighbors touch hands

Market, Chichicastenango, Guatemala

and whisper greetings. Worn metal scales glint in the morning sun as fingers flash tallies in multiples of five. An elderly couple, plainly fallen on hard times, try to sell their wedding rings. They stand near a knot of tethered piglets whose sale will mean more purple yarn, a baby's baptism, a new straw mattress, or perhaps a carved pine coffin. Beyond the bargaining and this whitewashed jewel of a church with its twisted columns and curling stucco vines, we recognize all five colors of the Maya cosmos in ears of corn drying on the tile roofs of Zunil's adobe houses.

"*Francésasalemán,*" children shout as we descend the church stairs, tagging us as some kind of French-German fusion. A steady stream of petitioners flows in and out of this sanctuary, for those who come to market also come to pray. But after giving these *santos* their due, many will seek out a saint not welcome within these walls. In the Maya world, just as much worship takes place on mountaintops, beside rivers, or in caves, fields, and homes as before images on Catholic altars. Condemned by priests, such rituals performed outside the church date back to ancient times. They derived from the natural world and its cycle, which spawned a complex and crowded pantheon. Every Maya deity had four manifestations—one linked to each of the cardinal directions and colors—as well as many faces: young and old, male and female, good and evil. Thus evil was accepted as an integral part of life. Come the Spanish Conquest, many gods were lost, but the Maya retained their belief in ambiguous deities who could both cure and curse, comfort and condemn. When native converts transferred this dualism to Christian saints, horrified clergy chased the evil aspects out church doors. Ever since, shady virgins, dubious sprites, and murky saints have held their own, disregarding the rebuke of Rome. From San Pascualito Muerte Rey, the tiny, skeletal king, to San Desiderio, the dirty, one-eyed angel, Sally and I always try to track down their painted shrines and chapels.

Chief among them is San Simón, or Maximón, whose rites we have witnessed in half a dozen highland Guatemala villages. Though Maximón looks a bit different from town to town, he usually appears as a life-size, cigar-chomping, mustachioed wooden mannequin wearing a dark suit, scores of scarves, black boots, sunglasses, and a wide-brimmed felt hat or two. He moves annually from house to house for his board and care. Maximón's name recalls his origins in the Maya Earth Lord, Maam, or "Grandfather"; the Christians'

San Simón, or Simon Peter; *maax,* the monkeys that are believed to be amoral survivors of a previous creation; and the smoking underworld deities, which may explain his addiction to tobacco. As both beloved healer and feared destroyer, Maximón is privy to petitions never laid before the sanctioned saints. He intervenes in down-to-earth arenas like quarrels, commerce, adultery, and revenge.

Today is our first visit to Zunil's Maximón. We join Frank, or "Pancho," an American Protestant missionary based in the nearby city of Xela, who comes to check out the enemy that he one day hopes to defeat. Only after joining hands in a ring of prayer will Pancho guide us to the home of this year's host. "Now God will protect us from the evil behind this door," he asserts. Passing the sentry, we enter a red, smoke-filled room paved with tiny flames, reeking of alcohol and incense, and crowded with supplicants and shamans. "Welcome to hell," whispers Pancho with dismay. The door slams behind us, making certain that Maximón's phenomenal energy does not escape. Bundled in layer upon layer of dark clothing, bright silk scarves, and wool gloves, the honored guest sits bolt upright in a green chair, holding a silver-tipped cane and "smoking" a Marlboro in his cigarette-stained mouth. "He looks

San Simón, Santiago Atitlán, Guatemala

smothered, doesn't he?" Pancho says, explaining, "Max must be kept warm. Heat is life. Only the dead are cold." After conferring with a guard in fluent Quiché, Pancho summarizes, "The Maya here say that Simon Peter, the first apostle, fell from God's grace and dropped right out of heaven into this tiny mountain village." Just then a woman suitor accompanied by a *curandero* approaches San Simón. She is laden with a carton of cigarettes, two bottles of rum, a liter of Coca-Cola, nine stocky black candles, and a bunch of

yellow bananas. "Max is greedy," Pancho declares. "Give him the right amounts of what he wants, and he'll do anything he's asked, good or bad. Black wax means big trouble. This color is used against enemies. She must think she's hexed."

The *curandero* taps his vengeful patient's candles against the saint's shiny boots before lighting them in a row on the dirt floor. Next he fills three small glasses with her rum. The first he swallows, the second he spills for the earth, and the third he swishes around in his mouth and then sprays upon his client in the form of a cross. While two guards tip back Maximón's chair, the healer pours the remaining liquor into the wooden mouth and adds the empty bottles to a small mountain of glass in the corner. "These witch doctors rig up a tube and bucket to collect the booze," says Pancho, shaking his head. "They sell it out back at an inflated price, since it's been 'consecrated.'" Now the healer takes the sufferer's pulse, asking over and over, "Does this illness have an owner?" as he listens to her blood "speak the problem." With this arterial guidance, he sweeps her vigorously with a whisk of rosemary and red geraniums and then rubs her body with two eggs to absorb the evil. "Later on he will set these eggs in a fire with rum and sugar," Pancho relates. "If they explode with a pop, that's a good sign. If not, look out, lady." Borrowing some of Maximón's trappings, the *curandero* sits the woman down, places a black hat upon her head, winds a blue scarf around her neck, and chants as he swings the saint's mighty cane in circles around her body. "These shamans talk mumbo jumbo," insists Pancho, "all about numbers and colors, lightning, mountains, and lakes. Max is served by the most important healers. They think his presence gives them power. So do the fortune tellers, like that one by the door," he adds, pointing to an old diviner who rattles and reads cloudy crystals and blood red seeds on behalf of the young couple at his side. As a guard's transistor radio loudly boasts "fifty thousand watts of power" and then resumes marimba rhythms, the patient, now dripping with sweat, rests her head on Maximón's arm and cries. Pancho grimaces. "People believe in this black magic, and so do I. These heathen idols are dangerous. I have known an Indian in perfect health to drop dead just because he angered a neighbor who bribed Simón to settle the score."

Heretical saints are not the only trial facing the Catholic Church. Pancho himself is a thorn in its side as it daily loses ground to a second wave of conquerors, the *evangélicos*. Jehovah's Witnesses, Baptists, Methodists, Pentecostals, Nazarenes, Presbyterians, Mormons, and Seventh-Day Adventists: over 250 sects, denominations, and cults today ply their faiths across the Maya world. And now that there are Protestant Maya, the rest of the Maya call themselves Catholics for the very first time. Aside from questions about corn and children, we are most often interrogated about which faction we back in the new religious wars. Protestant missionaries first gained a foothold in the 1920s when they sought out those Maya who were either too successful or not successful enough to fit into their own communities. Conversion came with incentives like fertilizer, insecticide, and medicine. During more recent civil wars, when Catholic priests with their liberation theology were branded communist, Protestantism offered safe conduct through repression. Today, the evangelicals' spirited services—with their clapping, speaking in tongues, conga drums, electric guitars, and saxophones all

Jungle Chapel, Las Metalias, Honduras

wailing praises to the Lord—fill pews with Maya who are understandably bored with centuries-old music and dance. But conversion changes much more than a Maya's place of prayer. *Evangélicos* are by definition *ladinos,* valuing families and their "personal savior" over the community and its saints. Suddenly their focus is heaven, not the village. And just as abruptly, economic success becomes a sign of spiritual grace rather than a magnet for envy. When Protestants reject the burdens of *cargo* and shun alcohol, they prosper and then testify, "It is God's will." Newfound wealth is then directed toward finer houses, modern clothes, education, and of course new, painted churches.

Like the Spanish padres before them, Protestant missionaries borrow everything they can from Maya belief to ease conversion. And just like those Catholics, Protestants first raise tall crosses and then build new—though less monumental—churches to proclaim "Christ's victories." These they paint in the sacred Maya colors, especially blue and green. While the Spanish only exploited *yax* in the cheap, jade-colored beads they once passed in trade, Protestants take full advantage of this color's rich significance. Today, in village after village they overtly co-opt the Maya's divine blue-green to symbolize rebirth in Jesus Christ and the baptismal waters in which converts are "born again." With more money and fewer restraints, Maya Protestants paint not only their churches but their houses, too. Sally and I have come upon many evangelical enclaves where every single house and chapel is painted blue or green, inside and out. For these young "communities in Christ," blue-green is more than just a color. *Yax* is both their history and their future as it draws on the past that it consumes with every brush stroke.

*Processional Carpet
Salcajá, Quezaltenango,
Guatemala*

All this change is too much for traditionalists. In the most extreme case, when the Protestant converts of Chamula spoke out against *cargo*, festivals, and rum and ceased contributing to their village, elders there sensed the ancient Maya fabric beginning to unravel. Fearing for the sun and its cycle, Chamula first ostracized its Protestants and forbade them to preach. Later, *evangélicos* were banished by the tens of thousands; their houses were burned, their lands seized, their existence erased. Exiled Chamulas now live in an ever-growing evangelical ghetto on the outskirts of San Cristóbal. Competing for the attention of unconverted Catholics and God, their loudspeakers blare from tiny, bluegreen "temples" with names like "Tree of Life" or "Jesus of New Waters."

Years after our date with Pancho and Maximón, when we are visiting Zunil for Holy Week, an old Maya man sums up the traditionalists' view of the schism when he explains, "The *protestantes* do not believe that the saints live. They say the *santos* are only stupid sticks of wood without heart or soul. They say we waste our money and our time. *Evangélicos,* they burn no copal, no candles. But we Catholics respect the Old Ones. We do not believe the words of the *protestantes.* We believe the word of God." He is interrupted when *cargo* officials in their tall, peaked caps and billowy black robes hurry toward the church with sticks of dynamite, fireworks, and a launching pipe, pulling a crowd and us along with them. At Eastertime in the Maya world, Christ is hardly the main event. The resurrection of the Son of God is overshadowed by clouds of the approaching rainy season. His victory over death has merged with the ancient planting festival that marks the reappearance of green life from out of dead, black fields. Lightning-like flashes and the thunderous report of skyrockets now proclaim that Zunil still holds to the old bargain. The air is thick with acrid black clouds of smoke, reminding the Chacs of their duty. Ash and debris rain down upon us. The host of saints just starting down the church steps for their Good Friday procession scurries back inside, out of reach of showering sparks.

Good Friday, Zunil, Guatemala

With our ears still ringing from the blasts, we follow as the *santos* reemerge to parade through the steep streets. Lined with the faithful, the way is carpeted in age-old patterns formed from colored sawdust and flower petals. These are soon trampled by the saints' bearers, who pass in a hypnotic haze of *pom*, reeling under their loads and liquor. A brass band in matching lime green shirts leads the way with a dirge, while boys swing six-foot wooden noisemakers to imitate thunder. Village elders sway before the images, shifting their feet in an ancient dance of prayer. A gas-powered generator, following at the respectful distance of its fifty-foot extension cord, provides flashing lights for a jade green litter bearing three "sister" Santa Marías, who endlessly weep painted tears. Meanwhile, Zunil Protestants have launched a howling strike against this Catholic draw with a preemptive chorus of "Hallelujah, Christ is risen." Paying them no heed, the *santos* stop off at this year's home of San Simón to mingle for a moment with their venerated friend, who still works his black magic in these green hills.

Shafts of thin morning light wash the yellow sanctuary of San Mateo Ixtatán in a pearl blue haze. Sally and I watch as a barefoot old woman shuffles to a side altar where a winged *santo* patiently awaits her prayers. As she ties a lily to a pillar with a piece of straw, we cannot help but notice her hands. Dark and lined, her gnarled fingers are adorned with five worn golden rings. She wears the long, thickly embroidered blouse of her highland Guatemala village; from beneath its brilliant reds, yellows, and blues she removes a woven pouch, fumbles with its contents, and extracts a few precious coins. Eyes fixed on the *santo*'s stare, she raps the rippled glass door of his jade green case with the edge of a silver piece, awakening him to her appeals before dropping each coin into the red tin offering box at his feet. They fall with loud clanks, the sound of heavy, old *quetzales* of small denomination. Reaching back into her pouch, she gathers a fistful of yellow corn kernels and spills them on the blackened altar.

In her Chuj Mayan she tells a fat candle what message to carry to her gods. Her crippled fingers strike one match and then another before they manage to light the wick. Joining other petitioners, she kneels stiffly on the cold tile floor with her arms outstretched and hands open to heaven. Her wails rise with the votive flame; though these ritualized cries of confession grow more insistent, no one takes notice except the wooden angel. Sensing that her apologies have been accepted, she regains composure and begins a circuit of the other saints; one alone cannot take care of every need, so none will be ignored.

Prayer, San Mateo Ixtatán, Guatemala

Bowing and crossing herself, she exits, kissing her thumb in obeisance before the sagging stucco church, grown soft around the edges from centuries of paint.

Later we spot this same woman selling colorful embroidery thread in the marketplace. A young man vending potatoes in the stall next door offers to translate, since Spanish is little known here. "She is Señora Magdalena," he begins. "She asks, in which valley were you born? Are you married? Are you Catholic? Where are your children? Do you embroider in your land? Do you grow corn?" When Sally reveals that she has produced no children, clothing, or tortillas, Magdalena cannot hide a look of gentle pity. I ask if I may take her portrait. "Not this wrinkled face," she moans, clearly flattered. But yes, I may photograph her hands, she says, for "these have embroidered much and attended my family and the saints, yes, the saints have been generous, and these fingers have given them praise."

Mounted, molting toucans, a splayed boa constrictor, and overstuffed, spotted jungle cats with droopy snarls and glassy eyes glare down upon our breakfast. These musty trophies—meant to lure the buses snorting between Belize and Cancún along the Yucatán's east coast— seem to dare us to sample the menu at this roadside eatery in the town of Felipe Carrillo Puerto. While ragged shoeshine boys work the aisles and even younger Chiclet sellers endlessly circle the room, a television alternates noisy snow with angry faces on the morning news. Ignoring them all, the mestizo manager sucks on a cigarette in the corner, his nose buried behind the lurid cover of a comic book. A lobster-faced German tourist who has evidently overshot the Maya ruins of Tulum shouts his order at the spiked-heeled waitress in the common belief that if he speaks loudly enough, his language will surely be understood. Just then, a tray of dishes comes crashing to the floor, and two Maya busboys, fearful for their jobs, set upon the shattered glass with brooms. Wakening to his duties, the manager strolls over to our table and apologizes for the uproar. When we ask about the nearby Maya villages, he warns us off with the universal sign for "slashed throat" and recommends that we keep to the main road. "The Indian

Bass Viol
Dzitbalché, Campeche, Mexico

*Dressed Crosses
Dzitbalché, Campeche,
Mexico*

rebels, the Separate Ones, they are dangerous, unpredictable. They are crazy with their crosses."

The Separate Ones he speaks of are the Maya we have come to meet. Also known as the Cruzob, or "People of the Cross," they are descendants of the rebels of the Caste War, the most successful native revolt in the history of the Americas. This bloody racial clash erupted in the mid-1800s, when dispossessed and brutalized Yucatecan Maya, led by fanatical prayer men, rose up against their "white" masters. In a frenzy of revenge, the rebels killed men, women, children, livestock, and even orange trees to erase all trace of their oppressors. Within a year these Maya had victory within their grasp. As the remaining Mexicans prepared to abandon the peninsula or die, flying ants filled the sky, presaging the coming rains. Mindful of their ancient obligation to the gods, Maya warriors went home to plant corn. Given time to regroup, the Mexicans retaliated with a vengeance and pushed the surviving rebels into the remote southeastern jungles of today's Quintana Roo. There, near a

Gilded Angel, San Cristóbal de las Casas, Mexico

small natural well just minutes from where we now sit, a cross carved in a mahogany tree began to talk. Such oracles were nothing new to the mystical Maya, who were accustomed to speaking stones, conversant corncobs, and visions of Virgins. Chan Santa Cruz Noh-Ca, or "Great City of the Little Holy Cross," grew up around this sacred symbol, which issued tactical orders for renewed guerrilla raids and prophesied victory for their holy crusade. For fifty years no Mexican risked setting foot within the independent Mayas' vast realm.

At the turn of the century the Mexican government, weary of the insurgents and undeterred by the many magical crosses that had since been carved from the original tree, stormed Chan Santa Cruz, renamed it for a martyred politician, and reclaimed the entire territory. Several thousand Cruzob slipped back into the jungle with their crosses, making this conquest as elusive as that of Tayasal. Today's Separate Ones, unreconciled to Mexican domination, contend that this era is merely an extended truce. Ever ready for military action, they await the final battle. Meanwhile Mexico has transformed their coast into the country's newest tourist mecca, where little that is truly Mexican or Maya need intrude on a two-week vacation. Now, sun worshipers marinate on inviting beaches, unaware that just a few miles inland rebels still commune with crosses.

Today the only monuments to Maya sovereignty are a scatter of tiny temples secreted within the thorny scrub. And so, despite rumors of Cruzob animosity toward all outsiders, we take to the narrow back roads, walled in by low jungle and the electric hum of insects. Eventually we pass the first double pair of blue-green crosses, sheltered beneath a small, thatched roof, that we know mark each of the four cardinal directions into every Cruzob village. A bit apprehensive, we pull up before a tiny church—just a slightly larger version of the simple huts surrounding it—brand-new and still unpainted. A handful of curious villagers approaches, hardly threatening with such smiles. Perhaps because the Cruzob believe we could never have entered this sacred precinct if the sentry crosses had not consented, they greet us warmly. Delighted to learn we are not evangelical missionaries, they are unexpectedly eager to show off their chapel of San Andrés Noh-Ca.

Entering the church, which is called *kukut* because it is "the body" of the village, we realize that we should have removed our shoes and hastily retreat to do so. The room is simply furnished with two long, worn benches; a pair of tall red candleholders fashioned from forked branches; and at the far east end, a raised platform draped in an oilcloth printed with succulent fruits. Crowned by a bamboo arch hung with fresh basil and leafy vines, this altar boasts a crowd of crosses. Each is cloaked in plain white cloth, with only red or jade green "heads" and "hands" exposed. "One cross for every family here," a young man explains. Dressed in the traditional white shorts and pleated shirt of his people, he is a *cargo* holder bearing his *cuch,* or burden. "Why are the crosses hidden?" Sally inquires. "Señor Santa Cruz is not hidden, he is dressed," comes the answer. "And do they speak?" I ask. "No, today they do not speak," he laments, "but they are still our way to God." These Cruzob surprise us yet again when they allow us to step up and enter La Gloria, or heaven, where the altar crosses stand; and they astonish us by raising the robes to let us gaze upon their painted "saints." There is not a crucifix among them; each is a *yaxché.* I ask if they will paint their church. "Oh yes, it will soon be as blue as the sky," a man replies. Taking our leave of these much-feared Separate Ones, we carry with us the vision of a blue church set in a green place at the crossroads of the world.

Offering, San Andrés Ixtapa, Guatemala

Church of the Speaking Cross
Melchor Ocampo, Quintana Roo, Mexico

EK

4

PAINTED CEMETERIES
SO THAT THE SOULS MAY SING

Death comes for everyone eventually, of course, but at this very moment dying seems all too imminent. Sally and I are sardined aboard a second-class Guatemalan bus that hugs a narrow dirt road high in the breathtakingly rugged Cuchumatanes Mountains. A black ravine yawns just below our open window. We are on our way to the village of Aguacatán to investigate one of the brightly painted cemeteries so plentiful in the northern highlands. But now the top-heavy transport—overburdened with ripening bananas, old bicycles, and a pink concrete sink—lists toward the sheer drop on our right. We and the other travelers consciously lean our bodies hard left, as if our weight and will alone could keep the bus upright. Sally nervously

Garden of Stones
San Pedro Jocopilas,
El Quiché,
Guatemala

OPPOSITE
Stone Skulls
Chichén Itzá,
Yucatán, Mexico

whispers that we may spend much longer in the graveyard than we had planned. As my eyes alight on the safety plaque mandating no more than forty-two passengers, I keep to myself black thoughts of the all-too-familiar headline in this part of the world: "Bus Plunges, All 100 Dead."

We had doubts about this bus as soon as we flagged it down, noticed its balding tires, and translated the maxim ONLY GOD KNOWS IF WE SHALL RETURN emblazoned across its cab. Now that we are on board, our confidence is hardly bolstered by the sound of grinding gears, the steering wheel fortified with duct tape, or the trailing cloud of oily smoke. Worry only mounts as we pass dozens of jade green roadside shrines and crosses marking sites where souls have departed this life in fatal accidents. At each dangerous curve and descent, vistas of steep, terraced cornfields—now dead and brittle as harvest nears—dart in and out of sight. Standing on the seat just in front of us, two small children chew on sugar cane and stare, transfixed by our light eyes and skin. Their mother, obviously a charcoal seller from her blackened hands, shields a bundle of red gladioli that are destined, as all flowers, for an altar or a grave.

Loud clanking sounds set off insistent shouts between the driver and his assistant. A flurry of exchanges then

Painted Bus, Olintepeque, Guatemala

erupts among the passengers. While we do not understand the Mayan admonitions, we can read the terror crossing faces. Turning around, we find that everyone in back is jumping out the emergency exit, abandoning baskets of chickens and sacks of onions in their haste to escape. When we see that Maya men, who would never appear bareheaded out of doors, are even leaving their precious straw hats behind, we know things are serious. Anticipating a fiery free fall, we anxiously join in the exodus. I recognize the Spanish word for "clutch" above the din. Babies cry, a woman

calls to her husband, and a burlap bag of limes spills its contents, further blocking the aisle. The bus screeches, shakes, and slows. A Maya farmer cushions Sally's leap to solid ground while I help the charcoal vendor down. She clasps only the children, her flowers forsaken to the chaos. The driver's assistant tosses chunks of firewood in front of the back wheel until the bus finally shudders to a halt. The sense of relief is tangible as we all stand at the cliff edge, peering down into the deep, dark gorge.

The driver does not seem at all surprised or shaken. This is clearly not the first time he has had a brush with death behind his fractured wheel. His bus—like most in Guatemala—is never full beyond capacity nor broken beyond repair. After U.S. schools drain the life out of old yellow buses, they are reborn here through gaudy paint, optimistic slogans, and ingenious patching. And so, scratching his ear, our driver lifts the huge engine cover and sends his assistant crawling underneath the chassis, armed with a small warehouse of spare parts. "Hey, I'm no mechanic," the assistant quips when he emerges, covered in dirt and grease. Reluctant to reboard the contraption, I ask a man how far it is to Aguacatán. Shaking his head he answers, *"Leguas, leguas."* I am not precisely sure how far a league is, but walking does not seem to be a reasonable option. Just then the bus starts up and makes a short test run, brakes squealing. Piling back on, men reclaim their hats, and everyone politely squeezes into their former seats. The remainder of the trip is uneventful, but on arrival we do not seek out the cemetery. Today we have come quite close enough to black Xibalba.

Sally and I never could bring ourselves to visit Aguacatán's cemetery on that trip or ever after, though we have worked in nearly every other graveyard across the Maya world. From these we have learned that to the Maya, cemeteries are places of transition, not conclusion. Death is simply another stage in the cycle of life. Just as the sun falls into the black underworld each evening to rise again with dawn, and just as corn dies with the harvest but contains the seeds of new life when planted in the black earth, so a Maya's death and burial are only the first steps in a long, dark journey toward resurrection. The cemetery that has taught us more than any other serves the Cakchiquel Maya trading center of Sololá. This town perches on a ridge overlooking magnificent Lake Atitlán in the central Guatemalan highlands. Each visit we make our way downhill from its bustling market plaza until we find ourselves within the sheltering walls of the place of the dead.

Sololá's cemetery, like so many Maya graveyards, resembles a tiny, fortified city, gleaming in bright colors and alive with activity. Its high walls—composed of tiered vaults housing hundreds of dead—enclose a sacred square of hallowed ground chockablock with tombs, mausoleums, and low earthen mounds. Within this model of an ancient city center, all graves perform as "sacred mountain" pyramids. Before them stand forests of crosses inscribed with names and dates, recalling the great plazas where groves of stelae once marked the passage of Maya history. Simple or stately, the graves orient east-west, encouraging souls to rise with the sun. All day long, women dressed as colorfully as the tombs come and go, tending to flowers and candles. Their loved ones' brief epitaphs are in Spanish, as few Maya learn to read and write their own language, but this does not hinder communication between the living and the dead. Crosses abound, opening up direct channels to spirits in the otherworlds, and from several quarters the chants of hired native

Red Column, Huehuetenango, Guatemala

priests rise with wisps of pungent smoke to comfort the dead while families look on.

Maya cemeteries like Sololá's are the focus of village color and creativity. At home, fear of envy exacts conformity, and in church, where extravagance runs no risk, individual fancies are held in check by sheer scale and community consensus. Given these constraints, a Maya may turn only to the graveyard to expend both surplus money and imagination. Here whimsy reigns as unique talents are safely played out in miniature on tombs. These often elaborate stucco fantasies—usually more substantial and better cared for than houses of the living—ascend like wedding cakes in an explosion of colorful swirls, cupolas, gables, and friezes. Their painted and molded flourishes may seem superfluous; in fact, they are imperative. Embellishing tombs safeguards village welfare. When a Maya death occurs, envy demands that inheritance be depleted; building and ornamenting a tomb quickly consumes the dangerous windfall. At the same time, this sacrifice fulfills a sacred obligation to honor ancestors and thus ensures their guidance.

Sololá's cemetery does depart from tradition in one noticeable way, however. It is located south of town rather than west—the Maya direction of death. On our first visit, while speculating over its odd location, Sally and I were startled by a scraping sound coming from somewhere overhead. There, a young Maya tomb builder was troweling cement to add yet another story to an already six-level family sepulcher. Calling out the standard cemetery refrain, "Have you people in this soil?" he soon appeared before us looking like a psychedelic cowboy in the wildly multicolored, country-and-western-style woven garb of Sololá men. We told him that we were here to see the beautifully painted tombs. "Yes," he said. "We Maya

Tomb Builder's Hands
Sololá, Guatemala

Towering Crosses
Romerillo, Chiapas, Mexico

*Layered Color
Muna, Yucatán,
Mexico*

prefer colors in death, just as in life. But the rich, their bones lie in white houses of stone and marble." "Why are there no black tombs here?" I asked. He thought a while and then replied, "Black is a sad color, the color of fear. No one would consign a soul to God in black." Before he hurried back to his drying mortar, we inquired if he knew why the cemetery had been built on this site. "So that the dead can see," he asserted, motioning toward the three grand volcanoes that had created and now ring the sublime lake.

Lakes and mountains figure largely in Maya belief. Any pool of water—from a bowlful to the sea—can serve as an intersection between the world of the living and the realms of the dead. Water's dark depths grant glimpses into Xibalba while its surface reflects clouds in the heavens. A mountain also provides access to the otherworlds. Indeed, the Maya believe that the First Ancestors reside within mountains whose peaks climb into the heavens and whose caves and craters lead down into the underworld of journeying souls. Where a mountain meets a lake is an especially potent junction.

Green Niche, San Mateo, Guatemala

Sololá's cemetery, placed to the south of town in full sight of both, acts like a gigantic *yaxché* linking those on earth with the gods and ancestral spirits.

Discourse with the mighty First Ancestors who dwell in the mountains is vital to community health. But dialogue with familial ancestors—the recently deceased now awaiting rebirth—is just as critical, because they are responsible for the well-being of their own descendants. Souls who have not deviated from tradition while living on earth attain the exalted rank of ancestor after four arduous years navigating the nine levels of the underworld. They then arise in the night sky as shining stars to join the great, luminous pool of human, plant, and animal souls kept by the First Ances-

tors for future use. There they remain for as long as they last lived on earth, growing ever younger as they advise and protect the living, who in turn care for them. Eventually, an ancestor will be reborn as a baby of the opposite sex into the same family lineage, perpetuating a beautifully balanced cycle entwined with that of the natural world.

Lakes, mountains, and crosses are not the only shortcuts to conversation with the otherworlds. Color, too, eases passage. In Sololá and throughout the Maya world, precious *yax* is the color most frequently painted on tombs, since it designates water, growing corn, and thus life itself. To the early Maya, the fertility of *yax* was manifested in jade. As the hardest stone known in ancient Mesoamerica, jade also signified permanence. Today there is still no better color with which to cloak the grave of a loved one bound for the afterlife. Jade green affirms that they are treasured, sustains them on their hazardous journey through black death, and signals their soul's eventual rebirth. The many Maya cemeteries that have no view of a sacred lake or mountain need not despair. They, too, can draw on these powerful aids if just a little blue-green "water" is brushed upon their "sacred mountain" tombs.

The color red also denies death. In ancient times, blood sacrifice kept the sun rising, and red pigment—once cast over the dead and still painted on graves—endures as a symbol of new beginnings and rebirth. Yellow, the third most prevalent cemetery paint, was strongly associated with death by the post-Classic Maya; they were influenced by the Toltecs and Aztecs, who believed that the underworld lay somewhere to the yellow south. At the time of the Spanish Conquest, Maya were still staining themselves with yellow dye to express mourning, and yellow marigolds

Girl, Green Tomb, and Volcano
Sololá, Guatemala

remain the favored flower for the dead. Together, jade green, red, and yellow paint on graves articulates affection. But these colors supply the journeying soul with even more. Through a lifetime of community service, a soul, which is born cold, slowly gains much warmth, only to die cold again. Descendants' offerings of painted color—along with candles, flowers, incense, and rum—replenish the heat so necessary for a soul's travels toward rebirth.

Tomb painting has long been a Maya tradition, as our visit to Kaminaljuyú, or "Hill of the Dead," revealed. The brightly painted burial monuments of this once greatest of Maya cities are now mostly buried themselves beneath the urban sprawl of Guatemala City. But enough has been salvaged from the meager ruins that remain to verify the care and color that launched the souls of Maya elite on their journey toward the starry heavens over two thousand years ago. A burial ritual there began with the digging of a grave resembling a stepped, inverted pyramid. Next, the body, draped in blue-green feathers and finery, was lowered deep within, dusted in red cinnabar pigment, and surrounded by offerings of jade, obsidian, quartz crystals, and painted pottery. A stepped adobe pyramid some thirty feet high was then constructed over this tomb and painted blood red. Together these two pyramids re-created a perfect model of the layered Maya cosmos. Positioned at the lowest level of Xibalba and warmed by vital colors, nobles were years ahead on their journey toward rebirth from the very moment of burial.

But it was back in Sololá that Sally and I discovered the one grave in all the Maya world that to us best illustrates these death beliefs. With a spectacular view of the lake and trio of volcanoes, this Maya tomb is painted a verdant green to conjure new life. It is accented with blue and green tiles and trimmed in blood red to speak of rebirth through sacrifice. Red scroll finials recall the ancient spiral symbol for smoke, the curling vapor rising from sacrificial fires that transmits messages to and from the gods, as does the jade green cross dominating the façade. Over the course of five years, my repeated attempts to photograph this glorious example of otherworldly communion had always failed due to weather. Finally one spring I optimistically set up to shoot this tomb for the eighteenth time. The early-morning overcast sky had stolen all color from the panorama, tarnishing the three towering cones with a lavender haze and reducing the lake to a flat, gunmetal gray. I waited patiently for the light to change. An hour later a young girl, wearing the colors of the Maya universe in her woven blouse, peeked around the corner of the emerald tomb. In that instant of epiphany the sun broke through, illuminating the slumbering crater of her Ancestors' home, now pillowed in white clouds.

An extremely persuasive toy salesman must have passed through Todos Santos Cuchumatán, Guatemala, since our last visit to this remote Mam Maya village. Now many of the *na* in this small river valley nesting high in these formidable mountains sport a colorful plastic rooster, elephant, horse, or spaceship. Wired atop the steep, thatched roofs, where they are curiously paired with house crosses, these "ornaments" oversee an eerie land of wind-stunted firs, cacti fences, and mammoth oxen dragging wooden plows through the farmed-out fields, which are spurned even by goats. It is late afternoon, and at more than eight thousand feet the air is cold and damp; so, after musing over the baffling new fad, we hurry into the sixteenth-century church for warmth. Primitive angels painted on the wooden ceiling look down upon a yellow room scattered with green pews. We pay our respects to the *santos,* who, though relied on for rain, are less revered here than an antique painted chest and its closely guarded contents.

Hearing a commotion, we step into the shadow of the entryway and see that a funeral is in progress just outside. Since the newly dead are not allowed within many Maya churches, the tiny, open coffin of rough pine has been brought only as far as the steps. In Todos Santos, as in so many rural highland villages where Catholic priests are rare, native prayer men preside over death. Today it is a baby's soul that the prayer maker introduces to the ancestral spirits

Stepped Stone with Hat
Todos Santos Cuchumatán,
Huehuetenango,
Guatemala

who dwell within this church. Tall, thin, and fine featured, he wears the uniform of the local men: red-and-white-striped trousers, black woolen chaps, a red-and-white woven shirt with a wide collar, a crocheted shoulder bag, and a straw hat with a low, rounded crown. His black wool jacket and advanced age mark his office. That he has survived so many years proves his power to withstand evil, and with his great heat he may touch the dead without fear.

Besides Sally and me, the only witnesses are an impatient young grave digger and the bereft mother. Her poverty and pain are immediate. She stares blankly, looking lost in a worn, once-beautiful hand-loomed red blouse. We hear a few words we recognize, among them "welcome," "child," and then "*sat-kan*" (eye of the sky), the Mam word for heaven. The mother does not cry, perhaps because tears could flood the baby's passage onward. Soon, she knows, her infant's soul will suckle at the sky's "Tree of Many Breasts," which always has abundant milk for every child who dies; rebirth will come quickly after such a brief life. When the prayer man sprinkles holy water on the embroidered cloth swaddling the lifeless bundle, the ceremony concludes, just minutes after it began. A church bell clangs once as the grave digger nails the coffin shut. Sling-

Archangel, Todos Santos, Guatemala

ing the wooden box across his back with a rope, he hoists his shovel over one shoulder and, without a word, hurries west uphill past a straggle of houses. The frantic mother half-runs to keep up.

A short while later Sally and I reach the cemetery, where richly painted tombs and a scatter of wooden crosses spill down a rocky hillside. Clusters of crosses disclose shared tenancy. Some have fallen to rot; the Maya say these should be allowed to age and die in their own way. At first the grounds appear littered with trash: old shoes, hats, belts,

hair combs, and the occasional knife. But these are actually possessions of the dead, forgotten in the rush of burial and only later dropped on top of graves where they become the property of wind and dogs. We easily spot the small mound of newly turned earth, sanctified with all the mother can afford: a single calla lily and a simple cross daubed with jade green paint. Like reverse Braille, a short, misspelled inscription has been pecked into the soft wood with a nail. It reads "*ninta*" for baby girl: too few letters to encompass so much loss.

"I paint all the time, because people die all the time," declared wiry old Anacleto Cobá Sosa Moó the first time we met. "Here there is always work. Always a gravestone that needs painting, always a new tomb to build, always bones to arrange." As "Official of the Sepulchers" in the Yucatán town of Hoctun, or "Many Stones," Anacleto admitted, "Some years I am so busy, I cannot refresh the flowers on my own family's tomb." The flowers Anacleto spoke of belong to a Hoctun color tradition unique in all the Maya world. As he explained, "You know, we have so little water in my village, the ground is stone, and the sun is very strong. Though we adore flowers, we cannot grow them here. That is why we paint the flowers to honor our dead. The custom is very old. Who knows when it began?" And so it is that this shade-starved cemetery blooms year-round with dahlias, roses, daisies, and mums in a veritable garden of painted petals, garlands, buds, and vines. Anacleto is chief among three artists whose floral offerings bring this rocky domain of the dead to life.

This year when we visit Hoctun, it is the week before the annual Days of the Dead, that celebration culminating in early November when the Maya and all of Latin America welcome their ancestors back to this earthly home. By the time the spirits arrive, the entire Maya world must be carpeted in flowers, blanketed in copal smoke, and ablaze with candles and fresh paint. Thus for Anacleto, October is the month when most flowers are planted with his brush. For thousands of years the Maya feast of the dead took place every August. When the Spanish arrived, Catholic priests looked for an acceptable way to channel the Mayas' deep devotion to their dead. The obvious solution lay in the Christian All Saints' and All Souls' days, which were in turn derived from pagan Roman mourning practices inherited from the Egyptians. These holy days meshed nicely with the Maya harvest rites of late October, the time when maize has died and offerings are made for corn's rebirth in next year's crop. The Maya had little difficulty extending this celebration of corn's cycle to people passing on toward resurrection.

As we approach Hoctun's cemetery gate, two men balance on a tall, wobbly ladder. Tossing cupfuls of chalky yellow-ocher paint, they douse the rough stone walls in preparation for this most important holiday of the entire Maya year. Anacleto, wrinkled from his fifty years of work in the sun, is busier than ever. He carries with him a long, yellowed list with the names and dates of those his fertile hands annually honor with flowers and inscriptions. He has much to do before the first of November, but he still makes time for us. As we pass among his works of art, Anacleto rattles off the clipped family names he has painted across tombs: Ac, Ba, Cal, Ha, Kat, Kik, Lol, Lum, May, Ok, Pech, Pop, Put, Tut, Yam, and Zic. "These talk of water, hoof, snake, blood, fruit, tick, soil, and stars," he tells us, for Mayan names all come from their everyday world. He also shares stories of those who lie behind each of his bouquets, for

Flowers for a Soul, Hoctun, Mexico

graveyard guardians are town historians as well. He is especially proud of the tomb that replicates the Hoctun church, others modeled after *na,* and several crowned with miniature Maya pyramids like those of nearby Chichén Itzá.

Anacleto stops before a pale blue tomb, once lush with pink, red, and yellow zinnias and asters. "This is my father's *osario* [bone repository]," he explains, a bit embarrassed by the peeling paint. Each year by late October, what rains do come to the Yucatán have robbed the graves of their colors. "Rain steals even the names of the dead," Anacleto says with a shrug. "In the old days I painted with chalk and pigment," he recalls. "Now I use *acrilicos.* These colors, they are stronger. They do not fade, but still they last only one year before the flowers crack and die." Sally asks him how he learned his trade. "I began painting when I was seven," he replies, "when I fell out of my hammock and cracked open my head. From then on I had the gift." But Anacleto did not paint on tombs until the year his father died. This ossuary was his first memorial. Just a few steps away, he stops again before a plain yellow tomb and points to its bare cement door. "It is my wife's," he says with a sly smile as he moves its heavy slab aside. "But she is still alive. For now it is my paint box." Sure enough, within her future resting place hide brushes, jars, and little cans of color.

Beyond this cemetery's walls there are no flowers. All that grows is spiky gray-green henequen, the only plant the Spaniards found that could be wrenched from the rocky Yucatán soil. Profits from the sisal fiber of this agave cactus built the nineteenth-century mansions of nearby Mérida. This same sisal rope tied the Maya to a brutal plantation system that offered nothing spiritual or nutritional to a people whose whole life revolved around corn. Anacleto tells

Pyramid Tomb
Hoctun, Yucatán, Mexico

us that the mighty landowners of Hoctun rest in the elaborate mausoleums near the gate. "They never touch the soil they own, even after death," he notes with irony. "But the poor," he laments, "those who have no earth of their own, they work in dirt all their lives and then are buried in it, too." With that he gestures to the low mounds at the back of the cemetery, where his flowers also thrive. "And for the poor," he continues, "even their final struggle with the earth comes at great toil. Here, soil is as thin as my shirt. For each one who dies, relatives must carry in fifty buckets of earth from wherever they can find it to help fill the stony grave." He goes on to describe how in Hoctun, as in much of the Yucatán, soil is so scarce that the dead remain in this precious commodity for only a few years before they are dug up to make room for another burial. The exhumed bones are then placed in small metal or wooden boxes inside family ossuaries. And so, in death as in life, Maya claim only what little space they absolutely need.

As Anacleto collects some paints to begin a new bouquet, we again praise the beauty of

Days of the Dead, Pomuch, Mexico

his garden. "If you should die in Hoctun, your soul will be happy," he promises. "But if you die in El Norte, Hoctun is very far to come for burial. Forty years ago one man did so, a foreigner. But his wife would not join him here in death, so they are parted eternally. She lies many mountains, many seas away. He rests here among the flowers."

Now that the Days of the Dead are here, Sally and I have returned once more to Mexico's Campeche State, our favorite region in which to observe this annual festival. With a name meaning "Serpent Tick," it is no wonder that Campeche is bypassed by tourists; but this unsung land of heat and stone holds a treasury of Maya color and tradition in its cemeteries. Campeche has had a long relationship with funerary paint. On its island of Jaina, the last land to the west in this western Yucatán kingdom, the late-Classic Maya maintained a necropolis for some twenty thousand souls. Excavations among the graves have brought to light magnificent pottery figurines, each a portrait offering painted in the five sacred colors. Campeche's Maya continue to paint for their dead. Sally and I are especially drawn to the cemeteries of three preconquest chiefdoms that survive today as a trio of neighboring rural villages: Calkini, Nunkini, and Pomuch.

The smell of turpentine and the smoke from burning weeds are thick on a hot wind. Despite the midday heat, Calkini's burial ground is abuzz with scraping, scrubbing, sweeping, plastering, and painting as villagers prepare to host the spirits of their dead. Scarlet bougainvillea spills over the walls, and the cemetery's paths are dappled with tiny purple blossoms swept in by the breeze. But nothing in nature can compete with the ornately painted tombs. "We summon the souls with prayers, offerings, and new paint. We call them with our love," tailor José Maas tells us as he slathers his family's ossuary with the blue of the sky. "The dead like the colors, and we like to paint for them." "Yes," concurs his wife, María. "We do as our ancestors. We tend to those who come to eat and drink. We clean and paint their little homes. Whatever we give with our hearts, they happily receive. And on their Days, we keep them company with joy, as if they were alive." José nods approval when I ask permission to take a photograph, saying, "You have come so far. The souls are honored by your visit and your interest in their colors."

Two Maya women pass by sloshing buckets of soapy water. They murmur greetings to José and María before stopping to talk with Wilbeth Chi Balam. Already Calkini's best *escritor* (writer), nineteen-year-old Wilbeth quotes his price to repaint their family name on an adjacent tomb and then returns to work. With the palm of his hand as palette, he skillfully letters a deep green antique-style script upon a turquoise mausoleum, where a fresh coat of paint has temporarily removed all history. He proudly informs us that his Yucatec name means "Mouth of the Jaguar," and that Calkini means "Throat of the Sun" because it is here, in the far west of Campeche, that the sun is swallowed each evening. His friend Jesús keeps him company this afternoon. Jesús admits that his own Mayan grows hazier by the day. "My head is full of Spanish, and English, too, because I work in Cancún. My family is *evangélico* now, but I always come home to Calkini for these days. We still respect our dead, and we will paint our tomb tomorrow."

Our talk is interrupted by hammering coming from a fancy monument nearby. There, an old Maya laborer in patched blue work pants welcomes my help hoisting a tumbled stone back into place. "I repair the tomb of El Jefe, my boss," he explains. "He has no one else." Fifteen years ago in the capital, El Jefe's throat was slit by thieves who were after his gold chains. Now this humble servant, devoted in life, remains loyal to El Jefe's spirit too. Across the way a young boy struggles to print his family's name in vivid red above the niche of a modest lavender tomb. Letter by letter he painstakingly copies from a crumpled slip of paper, striving to keep the inscription straight. Wilbeth knows this boy and tells us that ten-year-old Raymundo has been honored with the task because he is the first in his family to attend school. When he has finished, Raymundo shyly turns to Wilbeth for approval. With a smile and some leftover green paint, Wilbeth steps over and brushes a bold flourish on

Festival Notice, Oaxaca, Mexico

either side of his young friend's efforts. The ancestors will surely be pleased.

Paint is not Campeche's only draw. Sally and I also come here to look because in these cemeteries death returns our glance. The bones of the dead are everywhere. Skulls stare from darkened niches. A pelvis spattered with yellow paint pokes out of a green biscuit tin. Loose teeth sparkle from a votive glass, and vertebrae, ribs, femurs, and tibias crowd every polychrome ossuary. We know that long ago, wooden scaffolding exhibiting the skulls of sacrificial victims was a fixture of Maya public architecture, and that ancestral bones were once coated in plaster and worshiped at home. A similar exhibition continues today. When a soul completes its travels, descendants fulfill their sacred duty by resurrecting the dry white bones from out of the underworld's soil. These fleshless remains are then respectfully dusted off and poignantly displayed to pay homage and ease conversation, reminding all who pass of the profound cycle of life, death, and rebirth. In the cemetery of Pomuch this public display of those one step ahead on the journey is made even more personal because here, grinning skulls are often topped with wiglets of their own hair. Oddly, this sight, which would make both morticians and beauticians shudder, is quickly transformed from morbid to moving as we witness the living express their devotion. In Pomuch this means laying the bones of the dead to rest in a freshly painted tomb on a bed of colorful embroidered flowers.

"We paint and embroider so that the souls may sing," asserts Miguel Angel Poot as he reverently polishes the bones of his father in front of a sapphire blue tomb. "Yes," he continues, "our people in the dark must have new colors and new clothes each and every year by the second of November.

Pillars and Cross
San Antonio Sacatepéquez, San Marcos, Guatemala

Inscription and Shawl
San Antonio Sacatepéquez, San Marcos, Guatemala

With these they are contented." His ninety-two-year-old mother smiles in agreement while shielding her son's labor and husband's memorial with a huge black umbrella. We watch as Miguel gently arranges his father's ivory-colored relics in a small jade green box. Its white cloth lining has been embroidered with a lavish bower of red and yellow roses and the letters POOT in brilliant blue. Sally asks who created the intricate needlework, and Miguel replies, "My mother. Her eyes are cloudy, but she still carries out her obligations. She stitches all year to be ready." Miguel translates his mother's Yucatec into Spanish as she recounts, "Our village is poor, but all find time and money to dress the souls with beauty. They are our family. The flowers and paint we give the souls today will last all year. We honor the bones in this way until they turn to dust. As long as we remember, the dead will never die. But if we forget them, who will remember us?" Leaving the Pomuch cemetery, Sally and I spot a mound of last year's crumpled embroidery. Soon, without regret, these will be sacrificed—set afire to rise as smoke into the heavens.

On the road from the cemetery into town, business is brisk as villagers buy and sell special treats for the souls. Before there were cemeteries, ancestors were hosted at home; when Maya died, they were buried where they had lived. These dead dwelled happily beneath the earthen floor or courtyard, within earshot of their children working or playing above. Proximity ensured a constant supply of heat for souls and guidance for descendants. When the Spanish introduced the *camposanto* (holy field) and insisted that all dead be buried there, the ever-adaptable Maya began making regular visits to these preserves. To retain the former intimacy, however, Maya continued to honor their ancestors at home as well, and during the Days of the Dead they still fete returning souls by fashioning an *ofrenda* (offering) on or near the family altar.

The aroma of baking bread mingled with the spicy perfume of marigolds and *pom* accompanies us as we walk. Along this same road Maya kings once stopped to feast on grilled *pomuch* (flattened frog), which lent the town its name. Today the door of nearly every *na* we pass stands wide open so spirits can easily enter and consume the essence of the *ofrenda*'s generous array. A new father, Jorge Ucc, is one of many villagers who ushers us into his home to taste the delicacies laid out among his altar's flickering candles—one burning for each invited soul. Tamales, breads, tortillas, chocolate, limes, and tangerines summon the dead, while paper-flower wreaths, a heavily varnished carving of a child saint, a school diploma, two picture postcards, and a framed portrait of a young woman recall a loved one's life. This year their altar is dedicated to an unmarried sister-in-law tragically killed in a train accident just one month ago. A maiden, she is being honored today, October 31, along with the souls of children, rather than tomorrow, when adult souls feast. "We give her what pleased her in life," Jorge explains. "The dead never change their preferences. We will care for her soul for seventeen years." Rocking his baby in his arms, Jorge declares, "Just like my little son, the dead need us. No sacrifice is too great. The spirits, they arrive tired and hungry. We send them off well fed." Then, as if anticipating skepticism, he asserts, "The white *pixan* [souls], they do visit, it is true. Many see them, especially the children. We feel the spirit's touch. Candle flames rise when they enter and lower when they depart. Do not doubt. I am sincere. A drink upon the altar will be half-full in just a day. And though our offerings are cooked with much spice, they lose all flavor after they delight the souls."

The following afternoon a taxi carries us the six miles from Calkini to Nunkini. Our driver, Germain Colli, tells us that his village name means "Sunstroke" because in Nunkini the sun is very powerful. When we ask to be taken to the cemetery, he jests, "No, no, I will be going there in a box soon enough!" But when we tell him that we have no Days of the Dead in El Norte, he more solemnly responds, "What? Does no one die there?" Though Nunkini is just a hamlet, it supports two cemeteries. Along the rocky, unpaved road to Cementerio Sur, everything—from house façades and stone fences to tree trunks and the very ground itself—is freshly splashed with milky whitewash. "It is *joko*

Blue Tomb with Skull
Pomuch, Campeche,
Mexico

Soul's Gate
Nunkini, Campeche,
Mexico

[brightness], so returning souls will not get lost," Germain explains. On arrival we pay our fare and then join the swelling crowd of faithful among the painted tombs. A half-hour later we see Germain again, pressing the open mouth of a full bottle of rum deep into the red earth of a burial mound. Other bottles stand on end nearby, quenching the thirsts of journeying souls. Behind us a family reunion is in progress around a coral pink tomb. A woman sobs, her lips moving in silent tribute. We turn away to face a flame red stucco ossuary edged in flares of last year's lemon yellow paint. Its blackened niche, protecting lit candles and honored bones, closes with a tiny indigo gate. Perhaps the brown moth I see lingering on these deep blue slats is a spirit-come-home, for the Maya believe that the dead often return to earth as insects to partake of offerings. In order to avoid disaster, even flies and mosquitoes go unmolested on these special days.

Julio Azul, Nunkini, Mexico

Paper flowers festoon the arched entry to Cementerio Norte. The wasplike hum of dutiful descendants intoning prayers and singing hymns is nearly drowned out by the thunderous drone of bees attracted to the sugary gifts and pieces of broken fruit lying on the richly colored tombs. In a hundred variations on the theme of adoration, bright soda straws, aluminum cans, and shredded plastic bags have been lovingly transformed into the floral streamers now cascading across graves. Men hold their hats in their hands, reverent despite the cruel sun. A young couple, too poor to buy a brush, use their hands to hurriedly finish painting the family ossuary before mass for all the souls begins. Each time we stop to chat, we are invited to join families for *hanal pixan* (dinner of the souls), tomorrow's traditional meal of spicy chicken wrapped in banana leaves and baked in an earthen pit. From their questions we sense they feel sorry for us, so

far from our fields, strangers who know no one, with no people in this ground. As we continue to stroll, greeting and greeted in turn, we come across a touching tableau within a blue-green box: a couple, united in death as in life. Their skulls rest cheek to cheek, draped in lace cloth. At the trip of my shutter, a small, bright green frog jumps out of an eye socket. A good omen, the Maya would say, since frogs announce both the rainy season and new life.

Though only 9:00 A.M., it is already a twenty-iguana day in Yucatán State. As Sally and I enter the cemetery of Tekit —our third stop this morning—we interrupt yet another striped, yard-long lizard sunning himself atop a marigold yellow tomb. On our approach, number twenty-one scuttles across the blistering hot walls and slips inside a half-open aquamarine monument. Lots of iguanas always means an abundance of blue and green tombs, as if these colors alone could cool the bones within the ovenlike ossuaries. Wandering among the graves, we stir up grasshoppers and red dust, which is said to have received its color from Ix Chel's dripping brush when she painted East. We examine a wall of *osarios,* especially on the lookout for red handprints such as those we have seen in nearby cemeteries and on the walls of Maya ruins. Formed by pressing hands into paint and then against the tombs, these timeless symbols leave signatures of the living as brief letters of devotion to their dead. But here we find none. Our eyes sting, even under dark glasses. This is one of those April days when we wish the sun had decided not to be reborn. Instead, it is working double duty, glaring back at us from painted tombs. And so, when iridescent spots begin to twinkle on the monuments, we are sure it's a mirage.

Wall of Spirits
Tekit, Yucatán, Mexico

Matador
Tekit, Yucatán, Mexico

On closer inspection these prove to be polka dots of gold paint—something we have never seen before. We search out the caretaker, who is plastering a tomb. Bent forward in a stoop, his old body betrays a lifetime of heavy labor. His Spanish is as limited as our Yucatec Mayan. He answers each question with *"Yo no sabo"* (I know not), until I think to beckon him over to the golden dabs and ask, "Why?" Beaming a gap-toothed smile, he makes great flapping motions with his arms and cries, *"Ch'ich, papagayo"* (Bird, parrot). Then he holds open his palm, places his index fingertip in the center, and touches it to a dot on a tomb, repeating, *"Ta', ta'."* It seems the "paint" is a gift from the birds. Sometime, somehow, a local had discovered that the droppings of a parrot glitter like gold in the Yucatán sun. In this way, a bizarre but beautiful tomb painting tradition was born.

Unfortunately, the fine points of this custom, such as when the birds come, how the droppings are collected, when the paint goes on, and how long it lasts—much less its spiritual significance —are well beyond our pantomime skills. We do know that to the Maya, gold is the excrement of Kinich Ahau, so perhaps this paint serves to link souls to Lord Sun and his daily rebirth. Since the paint comes from birds, which the Maya call "the living colors of the world," perhaps this golden guano itself engenders life. Possibly the villagers adopted this paint because, as the caretaker gesticulates, "birds fly into the heavens like souls." We are still guessing when an iguana scampers past. Number twenty-two. At the sound of a horse's hooves, we all look out the cemetery's red gate, where a lean Maya cowboy slows his old mount's pace. Removing his cracked sombrero, he places it over his heart as he clop-clops past the burnt orange walls that wrap around the earth where

Gold from the Birds, Tekit, Mexico

his people rest. Like the gilt stars on the tombs, the reverence of his silent requiem stays with us to this day.

The first downpour of the rainy season is always an event, especially on the Yucatán Peninsula. The deep blue sky, marbled with white, darkens prematurely as billowing, charcoal gray clouds race overhead. Crooked lines of lightning crack and flash across the eastern horizon. The temperature drops as the roar of thunder rises. Frogs croak, limber palm trees yield to the wind, and clothes fly off bushes where they had been laid to dry. The air smells of water and ozone. This May the momentous afternoon appropriately finds us in Muna, or "Cloudy Water," a small town guarding the foot of the gentle Puuc hills that once served as northern capital of the Xiu Maya, the last Yucatecan rulers before the conquest. Looking out on the town plaza, we take shelter beneath an arched entry to Muna's great stone mission; its walls set with bits of ancient carvings, the church sits firmly upon the platform of the pyramid it quarried and now supplants. The shabby Circus Orion is in town, striped tent flapping. One of half-a-dozen itinerant shows roving the peninsula, its little train of rusty trucks carries exotic diversions to each pueblo for a night or two before moving a little farther down the old royal road. Orion's shaved ice stand—its line of deep-colored syrups sparkling like stained glass—has no takers in the storm. Rain hammers down as a boy does cartwheels in the deepening river of a street. Safe within an arcade, an orange seller's children sit inside a cardboard "boat" and hold up a sail of plastic sheeting to carry them over the sea.

We make a dash for the car. Drenched, we drive west to find the cemetery and wait out the cloudburst. Great white birds rise from the surrounding fields. The rain slows,

Scalloped Arch
Nunkini, Campeche,
Mexico

Roberto
Muna, Yucatán, Mexico

then stops, and we begin our survey of the painted graves. As usual, most are blue and green, with bones prominently displayed. We stop in front of an arched iris blue tomb crested with a cranium belonging to "Roberto," according to the letters just below. As I begin to adjust my camera, a robust voice booms from behind us, *"¡Muchos rayos!"* (Many lightning bolts!) Startled, we wheel around to find a tall, bare-chested Maya man in black trousers standing before a red monument. "I am Miguel Alejandro Farfan, the watcher of the graves," he announces with a broad smile. He asks, "Have you people in this earth? Are you here for the little tree?" We introduce ourselves, explaining that we come with honorable intentions and only wish to photograph the colors. Surprised by our interest in his charges, he jokes that we must have fallen from the sky with the rain. Walking beside us, he tells his story. "I am twenty-three years old. For six years I have served the Muna dead. Year-round I keep vigil, build tombs, and exhume bones. But the living, they must paint the tombs themselves. It is their duty.

"My people give tombs the colors of flowers," he explains. "In this way, if the living cannot visit every day, the dead still know they are cherished." Miguel walks over to some low mounds and says,

Corral of the Soul, Tetiz, Mexico

"These small hills with their crosses, they are children, little angels. And here, with the fresh flowers, this is a new grave I have dug. Do you wish to see the little tree of miracles?" Before we can reply, his small, thin teenage brother and assistant, Jorge, pedals up on a clankety black bicycle, having heard in town that two visitors have come. Explanations begin anew as we all continue the tour together. Miguel speaks of their mother several times, so I ask where she lives. Ignoring my question, he opens a simple aqua *osario*, removes a skull, and holds it before me with the blunt introduction, "May I please present our mother?" Unsure if the standard "the pleasure is mine" would be the appropriate response, I am grateful when he continues, "She has been dead for seven years. Our father lives, but he has sickness in his heart."

Miguel graciously grants me permission to photograph whatever I would like, and I work until another shower sends us all running to the little chapel near the center of the graveyard. Sally and I take seats atop a bare slab of concrete until Miguel mentions that this is where the dead lie waiting for the ground. He laughs heartily when we immediately jump down. Then, for the next several hours Miguel and Jorge reveal more about Maya death than we had gathered in many years of travel. "Our word for death is *kimi*," Miguel begins, speaking in patient Spanish highlighted with Mayan. "When *kimi* comes, the soul leaves through the tongue. It rises, so we must make a small hole in our thatch roof, yes, above the hammock, so that the spirit of the dead may escape." Jorge adds, "And in new houses, too, the ones of concrete block, we leave a tiny window near the roof." "Where does the soul go next?" I ask. "Why, to gather all the footsteps of their lifetime, and their sins," replies Miguel. "This takes time. Some people have journeyed far, even to the sea. So while the soul searches, we attend the body through the night with candles at the altar." As he speaks, I can see in his face that he thinks back to his own mother's wake.

"Then the church bell rings," says Jorge, "to tell all Muna that a death has come, that someone has crossed over to the other place, to *Mitnal* [Yucatec for underworld]." "Yes," confirms Miguel, "and in the morning the body is carried right here to this little chapel, wrapped in a white sheet inside a coffin. We dig the grave, for the same day they

Recuerdo Amarillo
Xocchel, Yucatán,
Mexico

*Tin Christ
Huehuetenango,
Guatemala*

The Remembered
Hecelchakán, Campeche,
Mexico

must be buried. I use these two sticks to measure depth and width. Then I fold the dead one's hands and close their eyes. I must shut the eyes or other deaths could follow. Sometimes the dead wish to see, and I must close them twice. Except for children. I leave their eyes open so they will not feel lost." Jorge tells us, "Many people come to say good things and say good-bye while prayers are said. Some whisper messages in the ear of the dead one because the spirits, they speak with one another. Then we sprinkle water from the church upon the body." "We do if I remember," Miguel admits with a wide grin. He laughs as Sally records even this confession in her journal.

"We bury our people with the things that served in life," Miguel recounts. "Shoes, clothes, a cane, a rosary, needle and thread, or their machete, and maybe a pencil, too, if they knew how to write. All these things I place around the body with the hair and nail cuttings from their lifetime. The dead, they must go whole to the grave. These things, they belong with the soul. The soul will need them. But we make sure everything is cut or burned or broken first, because these must be dead, too." "We do this as the old ones taught us," adds Jorge. "It is our custom." Sally says that we have heard some Maya will not be buried in sandals soled with tire rubber because these could inflate and burst in the afterlife. Both Miguel and Jorge laugh until they cry. No, they concur, they know nothing of this worry.

Though the rain has long ended, the brothers do not seem to mind that their work is interrupted by our questions. As Miguel reasons, "The dead are patient. They will wait." Again he asks, "Do you wish to visit the little tree of miracles?" And again, mystified, we only shrug. Deciding we are also patient, Miguel goes on. "We bury at sunset so the dead may follow the sun. I place the head in the west,

Wreath and Sky, Tekoh, Mexico

and then I cover the body with red soil. Now the soul journeys to *Mitnal,* yes, to *tan yol kab,* the center of the earth. This takes three years, maybe four. When the time is ripe, I remove the bones from this earth. For this I am paid sixteen pesos. All that remains is bone and dust, yes, for everyone the same. I place the bones in a clean white cloth so that the family may collect them for their tomb." I ask what happens if they are not claimed. "To dishonor the dead in this way would bring illness, yes, or death. Souls who are not treated with respect, who are not buried by our customs, or whose tombs are left untended, they will bring trouble to the living. They float above the cemetery. People have seen their angry blue flames. These lost bones, they burn and cry."

Once more Miguel asks if we would like to visit the little tree of miracles. This time he reverently bows to the crooked post leaning in the corner of the chapel. We now realize that both Miguel and Jorge have been nodding in its direction all afternoon. Our eyes opened, we finally notice the candle stubs, cigarette packs, and liquor bottles—as well as several bundles of bones—lying at its base. Suddenly it dawns on me. These objects are all offerings, and the wooden pole is actually a Maya god. "It is called *kojonché,* the miraculous little tree," Miguel explains. "Yes, inside a cave at a place called Yo Puuc in the hills about six kilometers from here was where our people found this trunk of the *chu k'um* tree. Nearby lay many ancient bones of the dead and painted pottery and special stones. That cave was a cemetery, too, and the tree watched over all the souls." Jorge adds, "When I was seven, the elders brought *kojonché* with ceremony. I remember well. Now it lives here to protect our dead."

The deity, smooth and tan, stands some five feet tall

and four inches across. Its base is caked with the cemetery's red clay because with this post, Miguel divulges, he must pummel the ground over each new burial. "I do this for holy reasons," he states. "While I pound, I speak prayers that send souls on their way." In a stony land where the dead have little time to turn to dust before losing their earthen home, this ritual seems wise to me; the tree-that-is-a-god serves to crack the casket and speed the spirit onward. In a hushed tone Miguel discloses, "This I do only after all have left. It is *k'ul*, sacred. It must be done in secret."

By now we have tarried so long that all the tombs, no matter what their painted hue, are dyed to brilliant apricot and plum by Lord Sun. Stepping outside to celebrate his splendorous dive into the underworld, we gaze as he transforms the sky from turquoise blue through flaming red to black of night. Jorge lights a few candles and talks of beekeeping and the region's famous honey. "I paint my hives bright colors, just like tombs. And they have crosses, too. These we carve in the house of honey just above the entry. When it is time to harvest, we ask permission first. I do not harm the bees when I gather their gift. I treat them with respect."

Red Vault, Isla Cozumel, Mexico

Miguel and Jorge shake their heads in disbelief when we describe the gray stone cemeteries in our country. It is unimaginable to them that we do not display the bones of our dead nor invite them back to our houses every year. "How can your grandfathers live on if you cannot see their bones? Are they remembered if you never speak together?" Jorge puzzles. "Here it is easy to talk with the dead. They live in their painted homes, and my brother keeps their vigil." Miguel admits that he sleeps here in the cemetery, and sometimes Jorge does as well; they keep each other company as they care for the sacred tree and the souls. We ask Miguel if he is ever afraid or bothered by the spirits. He roars with laughter. "After dark," he says, "this place can be as noisy as market day. I hear the voices of the dead conversing, but I have never seen a spirit myself." And then he laughs again. We thank them both and promise to return one day with photographs. As Sally and I walk through the cemetery gate, souls awaiting rebirth shine down from the sky above. We hear Miguel's hardy laugh echo off the painted tombs and cemetery walls. This sound must rarely die among the dead in Muna. Theirs is a place of color and laughter. There is no blackness here.

Pomegranate Offering
La Palma, Chalatenango, El Salvador

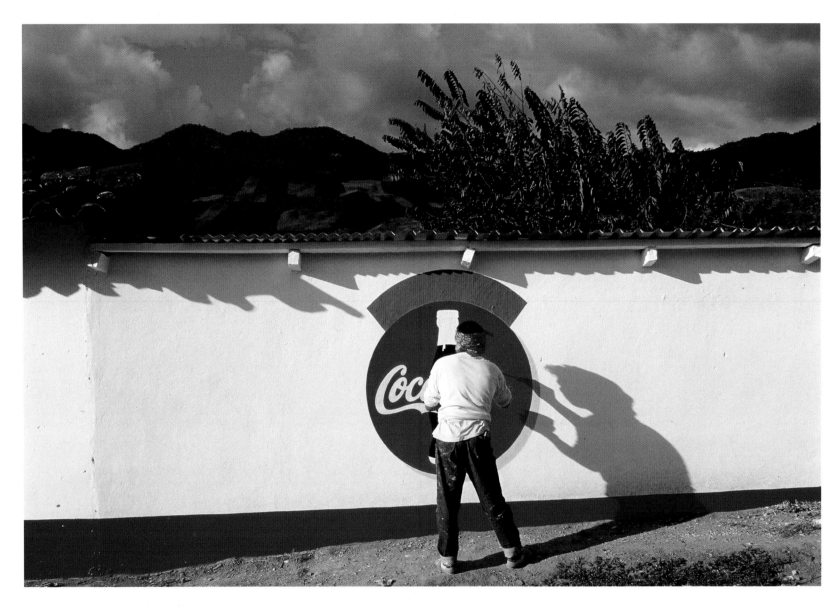

Maya Sign Painter
Bochil, Chiapas, Mexico

OPPOSITE
Faux-Feathered Serpent, Chetumal, Quintana Roo, Mexico

ZAC

5
CHANGE
THE FRAGILE WORLD OF MAYA COLOR

Profound changes have touched most of the people and places that Sally and I have come to know on our Maya travels. A road now cuts through a highland forest where a simple trail served well for a thousand years. A treadle sewing machine will soon shortcut the embroidery traditions of Pomuch. A satellite dish stretches the bounds of envy as it beams *Dallas* into a Kantunil hut. When we give a ride to three barefoot Lacandon boys hitchhiking to Palenque with bows and arrows for the tourists, the youngest turns up our Honda's air conditioner, punches on the radio, and declares, *"Buen coche"* (Good car). Old Anacleto despairs that some of Hoctun's young people fail to paint flowers on the tombs for the Days of the Dead; they dress their children as devils and witches and go to parties instead. At Christmastime in Chamula, the sacred east end of the church—the holy of holies—displays not a cross or a

crèche but a box of wildly blinking Taiwanese Christmas lights still arrayed in their Styrofoam packaging. On Zinacantan's main altar, a battery-powered bird sings for the *santos,* which are no longer washed in rose water for the faithful to later drink but sprayed with aerosol deodorants. And the nuns of Lemoa write to tell us of the "Coming of the Water," a new ritual with feast and fireworks to celebrate the villagers' completion of ten miles of trenches and pipes that now carry fresh water to taps all the way to the convent. Peace has at last been signed, ending Guatemala's civil war, and all over the country, missing villagers are showing up at mass for the first time in years.

The more time Sally and I spend among the Maya, the clearer it becomes that there is no real distinction in their culture between home and church and cemetery. All three are realms of faith, for religion is the center of Maya life. Since their spirituality is based upon maize, only if the Maya have land does their cycle of sacred colors hold meaning. Ever since the conquistadors' arrival, foreigners have siphoned off the best fields for private estates and lucrative plantations, leaving today's Maya with little soil to sow their holy corn and honor their contract with the gods. Without land to support their communities and families, Maya men are forced to labor in coffee and bananas far from home. Their frequent absence loosens bonds with ancestors, saints, *cargo,* and colors; their return launches the village beyond its provincial orbit. Traditional paint is inevitably a casualty.

Shortage of land may be the greatest catalyst of change to the Maya way of life; but other, new pressures are intensifying as tradition butts up against the technology, materialism, and pace of the twenty-first century. Evangelical missionaries prompt the burning of resplendent *santos* and

Farmer's Stone, Almolonga, Guatemala

the abandonment of both festivals and *cargo,* thus jeopardizing paint renewal. Lush rain forests are vanishing, and with them the birthplace of the sacred hues and home of the endangered, blue-green quetzal bird. The hyperactive travel industry splashes its Mayaland Hotels and Ux Malls with pretty pastel tints, wooing tourists with the promise of ancient ruins while enticing *milperos* to hang up their machetes and start opening car doors or skimming swimming pools. But war brings the most traumatic changes. Dictators, death squads, dislocation, and destruction all conspire against the Maya and their paint. Our documentation is lent a special urgency when houses, churches, and cemeteries fall to scorched-earth policies that also kill cornfields and poison the very waters of life. Armies understand the power of community and color when they push refugees into patrolled, plazaless, mud-colored "model" villages short on joy and bluegreen crosses. All of these forces disrupt the balance, reciprocity, and sacrifice that keep Maya culture alive.

Yet even the most traditional Maya see some change as desirable: communal corn mills eliminate hours of tedious hand grinding, shoes protect bare feet, and plastic water jugs are lightweight and do not break. These conveniences do not challenge old ways. But when prescription medicines from the new health clinic assure recovery, curing ceremonies fall by the wayside. When houses of mud and thatch give way to concrete block, Earth Lord cannot demand payment, so ensouling is curtailed. When pesticides and fertilizers provide abundant harvests season after season, the earth is no longer fed with prayer and sacrifice. When weather forecasters accurately predict rain, field rituals for the Chacs seem superfluous. Thankfully, such changes improve health, extend life, and lessen uncertainty; but they

*To the Coast
San Marcos,
Guatemala*

Sailors' Bar
Tela, Atlántida, Honduras

also chip away at the very foundation of Maya belief. As disaster and good fortune are accounted for through reason and science, trust in the supernaturals and fear of their reprisals waver. The saints are left to gather dust, and ancestors go hungry. The schedule of the clock supersedes the path of Lord Sun, and corn becomes a commodity. Such "progress" can never replace what the saints and ancestors grant: true harmony and peace of mind. We will never forget the Maya elder in Momostenango who lamented, "Our village grows poorer as it grows richer."

As far as the eye can see, vivid green banana plantations twinkle with chemical sprays and endless columns of coconut palms march in tidy lines toward the warm, turquoise waters of the Caribbean. Sally and I have seen little else all day while driving the northern highway of Honduras. At last we come to a cluster of colorful little houses not far from the town of Trujillo. Here, history has been made time and time again. Just offshore in 1502 an aging, disillusioned Christopher

Orange Stiletto, Zacapa, Guatemala

Columbus on his fourth and final voyage became the first European to meet the Maya. His ship's log records how a brightly painted, eighty-foot trading canoe paddled up alongside, laden with brilliant plumes, obsidian weapons, cacao beans, woven cloth of many colors, and some four dozen "civilized Indians" dressed in dazzling capes.

The chief merchant among these Putun Maya did not confuse the bearded men with gods. He signaled for the Spaniards to make way until he was at last convinced to go aboard, trade, and tell them of his land—"Maia"—and gold. Shrewdly pointing Columbus northwest toward the Aztecs, the Maya themselves headed due west—guided by

the North Star and Ek Chuah, their black merchant god—to make yet another lap in their thousand-mile maritime route between Veracruz and Panama. Ignoring their directions, Columbus sailed a few miles south into a beautiful, sweeping bay. Near the present-day site of Trujillo, his crew became the first white men to leave footprints and disease on Maia, the name they gave the New World mainland during their first mass to thank God for deliverance from *las honduras* (the depths). By the time of this town's founding little more than two decades later, nearly 90 percent of the region's natives were already dead from pestilence. As foretold in Maya prophecy, the great change to arrive on the white wind of the north was well under way.

Although Trujillo served as the country's first capital and port, the coast remained a backwater as Spaniards concentrated on mining the rich gold and silver deposits in the cooler inland mountains. About the time these veins petered out in the nineteenth century, change again arrived with whites from El Norte. First came eccentric Tennessee fundamentalist and filibuster William Walker, who declared war and attacked Trujillo in his quest to control Central America. But where Walker failed and met his death, the United Fruit Company soon succeeded. By the beginning of the twentieth century the bananas first planted in the New World by Spanish missionaries began ripening near Trujillo into this North American conglomerate. Labeled "El Pulpo" (The Octopus), United Fruit grasped huge tracts of Central American rain forest in its tentacles and stripped them bare to cultivate its "Chiquitas." To this day, banana leviathans hold landless workers hostage in "green prisons"; whenever rumors of land reform threaten, they protect their vast profits in "green gold" with the help of CIA-engineered coups and strong-arm dictators.

In the 1980s another north brought change to Honduras: Oliver North. Operating out of Trujillo's hilltop weather station on behalf of President Reagan's anticommunist crusade, North illegally funneled aid to Nicaragua's right-wing Contra rebels by selling overpriced arms to Iran in exchange for American hostages and cash. His covert scheme to protect U.S. economic concerns around the globe transformed Honduras into an army barracks. Human rights abuses multiplied as money, mercenaries, weapons, and drugs flowed through the country until our Congress caught on. Nicaragua was then left to settle its own war, and Honduras returned to the relative peace and pervasive poverty that today characterize the countryside, including this hamlet where we have just alighted. Its prosaic name, Kilómetro Treinta, declares a belief that it possesses no distinction beyond the fact of lying thirty kilometers from the next crossroads, but its colorful string of houses would have stopped Sally and me any day, even without the quartet of young boys luring us with live, bright green iguanas just outside their painted doors.

Balancing a pair of huge lizards across one arm, twelve-year-old Hector tells how he and his friends snare them by the river to sell to passing motorists. "Delicious for tacos," he describes persuasively, careful to avoid their claws while keeping a firm grip on the long, striped tails. Overhearing our talk, a banana worker en route home explains, "Ours is a poor country. We have no land of our own to grow corn or beans. Often there is no work. The government says these iguanas are dying with the forests. To sell them is to break the law. But a fat one like this, it may bring forty *lempiras* [U.S. $5], as much as two days' sweat in the fields. You understand, the boys must help their families, or they will have no food in their stomachs." Ironically, the very same delicacy Hector now hawks to truckers was offered long ago to Maya gods as fitting blue-green sacrificial fare. Just like these iguanas, Hector's Maya heritage is nearly extinct, his

blood and traditions joined with those of African slaves and Spanish overlords. He has never been told of the sacred colors and rituals of his distant ancestors, and the *chac* and *yax* of the painted wall he stands before simply mask the desperation. They hold no more meaning than the name of his village, this mere widening in the road without history, church, or patron saint. When Sally and I drive off, the fat iguana lies across the backseat, petrified with fright. We release him in a stream on the outskirts of Trujillo.

Much of the painted color in the Maya world today evokes not ancient gods and their sacred diamond but new gods of commerce and their seductive logos. With each successive trip Sally and I find ourselves solicited by more of this "commercial color." Whether Pizza Hut red, Dos Equis yellow, Pemex gasoline green, McDonald's golden arches, or the ubiquitous red, white, and green of Mexico's ruling party, these eye-catching colors now coat the cities and spill across remote village walls, spread by financial incentives or political coercion. In this land where *zac* (white) once denoted anything artificial or in a state of change, brilliant commercial colors now take on this role. Some of the modern hues ignore the old Maya symbolism, and others borrow from it, but all erode the ancient color lexicon, altering the painted landscape forever. Gaudy ads touting fluorescent orange soda insist, "Crush *es tu color*" (Crush is your color), but orange never was a Maya hue. Guatemalan billboards picture a handsome smoker posed before the Maya church of San Andrés Xecul, appropriating its rich yellow façade—dripping with plump red fruits, green vines, and jaguars—to trumpet "cigarettes with the taste of success," thereby equating *ladino* prosperity with the Maya's powerful colors and their old ally against fatigue and pain: tobacco. All colors—old and new—travel the Maya roads, where buses blaze with proclamations of faith. Portraits of Jesus mind the mud flaps, words of hope scroll across bumpers, and painted saints ride shotgun on the hood. Eager to jump on board are promotions for the holy "cola wars."

Boy with Iguanas
Kilómetro Treinta, Colón, Honduras

Yellow Façade
San Andrés Xecul, Totonicapán, Guatemala

As the red, white, and blue insignias of Coke and Pepsi invade Maya ritual, soft drinks are overtaking alcohol in the battle for market share. In an unorthodox campaign, competing soda distributors claim to *curanderos* that the more expensive the bottle, the bigger the burp—proof of evil exiting the body—and thus the greater their drink's healing powers. One afternoon in the highland Chiapas market town of Bochil, Sally and I spoke with five itinerant Maya sign painters working for Coca-Cola. Racing against time as rain clouds gathered over the corn-quilted hills, they told us it would take them five hours to complete this task before moving on. "We keep ahead of Pepsi," reported Rubiel proudly as he put the finishing touches on Coke's familiar, blood red sphere. Rolember crowned it with a jade green band, summing up, "Today Coke gets another sign, the owner of this wall gets new paint, and we get paid."

At least for now, it is still cheaper in the Maya world to paint signs by hand than to print and post them. The same goes for "political paint." Prior to elections, no boulder, fence, bridge, wall, tree trunk, or old tire is safe from candidates' color schemes. Predictably, Protestants choose blue or green to stake their party's claims. For all others, voting season is a color free-for-all. It is often said that with all their fresh paint, these politicians do more for their countries as nominees than they ever accomplish in office. When candidates lose, their painted promises are quickly whitewashed over. For the largely disenfranchised Maya, the victors' colors that remain sometimes signal death. Political persecution has chased thousands of Guatemalan Maya into Belize, where these refugees often bring their diamond cosmos back to life in a land that lost these colors long ago.

Directo, Suchitoto, El Salvador

Belize, Mayan for "muddy waters," was a crucial center of early Maya life. Some two million Maya once thrived here in more than six hundred cities, whose ancient buildings are still this country's tallest. With the end of the Classic era, when most Maya moved into the Yucatán, nearly all who remained in Belize—and survived the Spanish Conquest—were consigned as slaves to Guatemala, carrying their traditions with them. Over the past century Maya have slowly begun to return, to escape first Mexico's Caste War and then, more recently, the civil wars raging just beyond the borders of this former British colony. Democratic, English-speaking, sparsely populated, and armyless, Belize is odd man out among its Central American neighbors. Today, as Sally and I drive the rutted Hummingbird Highway through the lush Maya Mountains, we wave to bearded Mennonites in a horse-drawn buggy, a sooty crew of Chinese cane cutters, and a black man wearing a green satin shirt and pink curlers. These people and their town names—Teakettle, Chan Chen, Calcutta, Chicago, La Milpa, Nim Li, and Trinidad—tell of the many influences at play. But the boisterous paint establishes that Belize leans more toward Caribbean color than to the sacred Maya hues.

Suddenly, at Mile 25, we come upon a trio of wooden houses painted as green as banana leaves. Certain that this must be a Maya homestead, we stop. Approaching the first door slowly, as is proper etiquette, we are greeted by three little sisters wearing paper-thin cotton dresses. Speaking a jumble of English and Spanish, Lidia, the eldest, confirms that her family and two others left Guatemala a dozen years ago, just before she was born. I picture her parents forced to flee the violence in their ancestors' mountains and follow

Sign of the Revolution
Cojutapeque, Cuscatlán, El Salvador

Vota
Constitución, Quintana Roo, Mexico

Refugee's House
Maya Mountains, Stann Creek District, Belize

ancient paths to this strange, raw frontier. Here, on this tropical hillside, they cleared a square of jungle to plant their corn. Though they abandoned their thick, woven clothing in the heat, they had obviously carried their colors with them, including the carved Maya figure painted red and nailed to this green door.

Hearing a throbbing reggae beat, we turn to find Lidia's older brother, Eliseo, returning from his milpa with a radio and hoe. He is old enough to remember the terrifying climb down out of the highlands, the weeks on the run, and the border crossing. "In our old village," he relates, "I helped mix red mud, the reddest we could find, to build our house, but we made this house from wood, like all the others here. We can no longer pray at our old church. Our parents, they say they miss the *santos*. So for them I have painted our house the green of the old church, to remember. My mother says this color, it is her solace, her inspiration."

Sally and I have yet to find a village in El Salvador beyond sight of a volcano or the suffering that belies the "salvation" of this country's name. The land itself is wounded, the architecture destroyed, and the people broken physically and spiritually by a twelve-year civil war only recently ended. But this was not the only violent change to wrack El Salvador in the twentieth century. In 1932 over a thousand years of Maya culture all but disappeared here with "La Matanza" (the Massacre). When natives rose up to recover stolen land, the military dictator of that time ordered every man in traditional clothing killed and every Indian village leveled. Some 30,000 peasants were forced to dig their own graves before being shot. Dress, languages, and customs evaporated over-

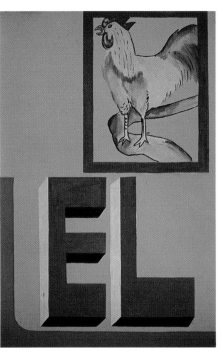

El Gallo, Orange Walk, Belize

night. Children may still be told that their grandfathers were once Maya, but now, for their health, all are *ladino*. As a result of La Matanza and the recent civil war, today's red paint speaks more of communism than of sacrifice to the gods, and black speaks everywhere of mourning. Color, swinging free of tradition, now hides the scars of war or tags the teeming gray capital and its shantytowns in gangland hieroglyphics. Where the paint of choice sprays from cans, I find little to photograph.

Sometimes I encounter powerful images that can be preserved only as memories. My camera would intrude. One afternoon upon a hillside in western El Salvador, such an icon unexpectedly appears. Halfway between the ruins of Joya de Cerén and the village of Izalco, where La Matanza first erupted, Sally and I stop along a trail to observe an old man. With his classic Maya profile in marked contrast to his chino pants and cotton shirt, he stands as still as a statue in the center of a fire-blackened field near a small blue cross and a wisp of rising smoke. As biscuit-shaped clouds scud overhead, he slowly bows to the four directions and calls on the power of their sacred colors, preparing to make milpa in the old way. Though we cannot hear his murmured prayers, we have witnessed this ancient rite throughout the Maya world. We know he must be calling to the Earth Lord in Spanish; ever since the Massacre, his gods have also had to learn a foreign tongue. While he toils, he surely cries like all *milperos,* "Forgive me, for I mean no malice. Though I trouble your soul, I only do as my people have always done, so that I and my family might live. I only pierce your beautiful skin so I may plant my seeds. May I borrow your soil for a season? I have need." And so this old Maya, bereft of all but this ritual, continues to fulfill his obligations to the earth and its cycle. In a graceful dance choreographed by nearly forgotten forefathers, he steps forward, pressing his digging stick into the black soil at the same time as he removes a few golden kernels from a woven shoulder bag. Bending down as if curtsying to the earth, he funnels these seeds into the small hole he had opened with his previous chassé. He does not waste a motion. Rising, he slides his foot back to bury the precious life, lifts his stick, and then glides forward again, each step a benediction.

The Maya wheel of time will soon complete another great round. When Lord Sun begins his rise out of the depths of winter solstice to commence his journey northward in the year 2012, one hundred life spans—5,200 years—will have passed since the creator gods first molded man from corn. Even though commemoration of the Long Count ceased over a millennium ago, the living Maya somehow know that this momentous date draws near. For them December 23, 2012,

Tomb Painter's Palette, Calkini, Mexico

will not necessarily mark a cataclysmic finale but rather a completion of prophecy and a new beginning. The Cruzob Maya say that with this new era Chichén Itzá, its ancient rulers, and a feathered serpent of stone will come alive, leading the Separate Ones either to bloody triumph over the Mexicans or to final defeat, the end of this Creation, and the birth of a new, more deserving race of men. In another revelation of the coming change, Lacandon Maya predict that this day's dawn may herald the sound of the last remaining tree to come crashing to their forest floor. Since the roots of all living things are tied together, when that tree falls, so will the stars. Then all Lacandon will gather at the ruins of Yaxchilán, where Tsibatnah, the god of art who first painted ancient cities like Bonampak, will hang unmarried Maya by their heels, cut off their heads, and drain their blood into clay pots. With this red sacrifice, Tsibatnah will paint the sacred cities back to life.

The Maya are not alone in predicting their future. Ever since Spaniards brought change to these shores, the world has repeatedly written the Maya epitaph. But to the Maya, change has never meant the end. Maya forefathers ignored the Europeans when possible, adapted when unavoidable, acquired when beneficial, and rebelled whenever the foundation of their colorful cosmos was at risk. Though sustaining great wounds, the resilient Maya endure. Today their numbers are actually increasing and, through the efforts of such courageous champions as Quiché activist and 1992 Nobel Peace Prize recipient Rigoberta Menchú Tum, so is awareness of their past glories, present struggles, and fragile future.

While much has changed in the Maya world since the Spanish Conquest, the Maya majority unfortunately remain at the bottom of the Mesoamerican pyramid, where they continue to be viewed as a threat to the ruling minority on top. Poverty and injustice still decimate like plagues of old, and the chronicle of human misery only grows. We have watched Maya street children sift through garbage, their torments dulled by the fumes of cobblers' glue; some raise babies of their own now, another generation without hope. We have seen a young Maya man flee at the sound of our car's approach in the lane near his home, where other strangers had unleashed unimaginable terrors. We have been told about the first-class bus that did not stop because it was only a Maya woman it had struck. We have heard firsthand a civil war refugee's nightmares, which replay her children's grisly murders. And we have read that Guatemala's peace treaty grants amnesty to those responsible for thirty-six years of horrors and so breaks the promise of "no impunity" that the Lemoans carved in stone to their dead. Sadly, we know that our own government trains and finances much of the vicious machinery of Maya oppression, thus contributing to the greed, corruption, and atrocities that so often transform the radiant Maya culture of colors into one of fear, hunger, and death.

Whether this book records a fading or vital color legacy, we cannot know. But we are certain that at this very moment somewhere in the Maya world, a shepherdess greets the red dawn, a road worker finds time to plant golden corn, and villagers still pray for black clouds to bring rain to their fields. We know that somewhere a *cargo* official touches up the carved robes of a *santo,* while a dutiful son paints a cross jade green to keep in touch with his mother. And we are encouraged to find that as Maya scatter to the four directions, they take their colors with them. Like ancestral souls who pass from the cool, dark room of the underworld to shine in the heavens as stars, the five sacred colors may suffer trials but live on, guiding the Maya on their journeys through the east, west, north, south, and blue-green center of the world.

Blue-Green Angel
San Cristóbal Totonicapán, Guatemala

ACKNOWLEDGMENTS

Meeting *Maya Color*'s challenge—to create a single volume out of ten thousand images and two thousand pages of field notes gathered across five countries and eight years—would not have been possible without the help of a great many people. First, we thank our parents, John and Viola Aberg and Bill and Jackie Becom, who each in their own way inspired us to seek, study, and persist.

Next, we extend our deepest gratitude to Norman Laboe, Roger and Marion Swaybill, Morley and Frances Baer, Robert Locke and Timm Crull of Watermark Press, and Douglas Abbey, Robert Burke, and Hamid Moghadam of The AMB Companies for nearly two decades of unswerving confidence and unceasing support.

We also wish to express our sincere appreciation to those fine art photography representatives whose integrity and enthusiastic efforts have given us the freedom to complete this labor of love: Margaret Weston and Matthew Weston, Carmel, California; Catherine Edelman, Chicago; Yancey Richardson, New York City; Susan Spiritus, Newport Beach; Ted Streshinsky and Photo 20-20, San Francisco; Gail Gibson and Claudia Vernia, Seattle; and Lee Marks, Shelbyville, Indiana. We look forward to equally long-term relationships with Robert Klein, Boston; John Cleary, Houston; and Peter Fetterman, Santa Monica.

Robert Abrams, Mark Magowan, and Myrna Smoot of Abbeville Press showed early faith in *Maya Color* by securing a simultaneous French edition with Editions Abbeville in Paris and then placing our project in the gentle but meticulous hands of Jacqueline Decter—every writer's dream editor—and those of the renowned Nai Chang—every artist's dream designer. We are indebted to them all for their guidance and vision. We are also fortunate to have had the inestimable counsel of Laurie Fox of the Linda Chester Literary Agency.

The images in this book could not have been reproduced with such fidelity without the extraordinary talents and painstaking care of Paul Mason, Sara Herrett, Mary Beth Wilkes, Tina Wiseman, and especially Esse Carol Anderson Lyle. Our hats are also off to David Azose and the entire crew at Ivey Seright International, as well as to Iris Photographic, Red Shoes, and Fry Photographics.

We reserve special praise for our "other eyes," those priceless friends who, image by image and page by page, shepherded the merging of this book's many voices at the same time as they helped us find our own: David "All Over the Map" Jouris, Lucas Blok, Barbara Ruzicka, Heidi Aberg Long, and Jerry Long. Linda Goldman, Dennis Love, and Mona Nagai kindly assisted in photograph selection.

Following are the teachers, travel companions, scholars, research centers, government agencies, and "lifesavers" whose assistance and encouragement were vital to the making of this book:

BELIZE Dr. Henry W. Anderson, Stephanie Diane Anderson, and Harriot Topsey.

EL SALVADOR Magdelena Chicas, Instituto Salvadoreño de Turismo, Arquitecta Doña María Isaura Arauz, Francisco Ponce Escalante, and Eddie Teresa Castro.

GUATEMALA Teresa Alonzo Chumil, Victor Alonzo Pocop, Octavio Alva Gramajo, Cecilia Ayala, Charles Banta, Dr. Boris Castillo C., Antonio Chavez, Anna Chay, Eluterio Chay Quiej, Mario Cohn, Madeline Colindres, Marco Antonio Contreras, Hotel Spring, Instituto de Antropología e Historia, Instituto Guatemalteco de Turismo, Don Juan Lopez Sanchez, Miriam A. Marquez, the Maryknoll sisters of San Sebastián Lemoa, Julio Miralbes R., Dr. Italo Morales, Arquitecto Marco Tulio Ordóñez, Guillermo Padilla, Victor Peréz, Julian Pocop Ramos, Nicolás Ramírez Sojuel, Héctor Solís Siliezar, Jean Swanson, Kathryn Topke, and Francisco Valladares.

HONDURAS Ricardo Agurcia Fasquelle, José Davíd Chinchilla, Rosemary Collie, Professor Oscar Cruz M., Max Elvir, Julio Garcia Santos, Hacienda El Jaral, Instituto Hondureño de Antropología e Historia, Instituto Hondureño de Turismo, Doctora Olga Joya, Embajadora Nadina Lefebvre Labro, Fronica Johanna Miedema, Israel Núñez Pavón, Desideria Perez, Rachel Rankin, and Angel Zamora Cruz.

MEXICO Paula Bidle, Calidad Total, Familia Candido, Arquitecto Miguel Cárdenas Barrera, Felipe Chapus Obando, Ruth Chojnacki, Manuel Cosío, Gertrude Duby Blom, Herb and Carla Felsted, Marcelino Luis Gómez Martinez and "Las Estrellas," Enrique Gonzales Ruffini, Damien Gutierrez, Mercedes Hernández Gómez, Instituto Nacional de Antropología e Historia, Arquitecto Ricardo Legorreta, Gregorio Luke, Raymundo Lorenzo Manzanilla Lopez de Llergo, Rosario May Lopez, José Rafael and Rosa Mazadiego del Valle, Javier Mendez Alvarro, Mexican Cultural Institute, George "Bud" Moore, Candelaria Moreno Hernández, Arquitecto Armando Moreshi L., Na-Bolom, Kippy Nigh and "La Casa del Pan," Patrizio Ortíz González, Carmen Ramirez Degollado, Doctora Carmen Ramos Ozona, Mario Roman Sanchez, Jose Gerardo Santiago Perez, Carlos Silva Rhoads, Malú Suárez B., Clara del Carmen G. Torres, Familia Jose Torres, Yosefa Ugav, Anna Utech, Familia Vivanco Ruiz, Carlos Lorenzo Vives Iñiguez, and Vivika Wahlin.

UNITED STATES OF AMERICA, CANADA, AND ENGLAND Susan Aberg, Lauren Adams Allard, Anton Agalbato, The American Architectural Foundation, Amnesty International, Ansel Adams Center for Photography, Thomas Anson, Elaine Osmunson Arnt, John Barber, Christian Barthod, Rick Barot, Kay Bartlett, Tom and Ellen Bauch, Sheila Berger, Howard Besser, Judy Bloch, Jay and Remie Bontrager, Stephanie Boris, Ben Box and the *Mexico and Central American Handbook,* Douglas Bradley, James Frederick Brady, Barbara Brown, David

Calamari, Terry Calen, Robert and Joyce Caproni, Tom Carlisle, Center for Photographic Art, Linda Chester, Dave Christensen, Cletus Collins, Susan Conrad, Ina Cooper, John DePrez, Rick Deragon, Kevin and Suzanne Duggan, Eastman Kodak Company, Mel Edelman, Rob and Joy Ellis, Alice Erb, Kathy Erickson, Amy Essick, Betsy Evans, William K. Everson, Pat Fauth, Dr. Edith Fiore, Yolanda Fletcher, Ann Flournoy, Gerry Fox, Mark and Bambi Fox, Julie Frederickson, Leonard Frizzi, Richard Gadd, Father James Geoghegan, Kathy Geritz, Drew Goings, Señor Gold, Paul Goldberger, Linda Goodwill, Pilar Graves, Mary Reese Green, Christopher Grimes, Guatemala News and Information Bureau, Celso Guitián, Diane Gysbers, Linnea Hamer, Mark Neiman Hammer, Patricia K. Harris, Piers and Carol Haslam, Marty Hastings, Holly Haynes, Phoebe A. Hearst Museum of Anthropology, Jon Heminway, Peter Hemp, Donald Henderson, Dennis High, Pennie Fenton Hink, Randy and Barb Hirtzel, John and Maxine Hoff, Lewis and Judy Hoff, David Hoffman, Steven and Cathi House, Bob Howard, Catherine Hudson, Michael Hutchinson, Anne Irving, Dr. Susan Jacobson, Gary Jaffe, Dr. Z.F. "George" Jaworski, Stefanie Kaku, Gary Kent, George and Sally Kiskaddon, Stephen and Kathy Koch, Barbara Kornstein, Edith Kramer, Charlotte Kroll, La Peña Cultural Center, Jon and Wiebke Larson, Stacia Leech, Bill and Elaine Levin, Claus Levinsen, Mark Levinson, the libraries and librarians of the University of California at Berkeley, Nelson Lindley, Robert and Kathie List, Tim Lippert, Suzy Locke, Amy Goldstein Lord, Charles Loving, Jeffrey Lyle, Robin Renee Maus, Dan "Stressed Plant" May, Dug McCallister, Linda McDougall, David Scott Meier, Roger Meredith, George Miers, Monterey Peninsula Museum of Art, Steve Moriarty, Mary Murray, Karen Nagano, Avon Neal, Emily Novak, The Octagon Museum, Scott Olson, Robert "Optima" Pace, Ann Parker, Ginny Perkins, Peter Pfersick and Looking Glass Photographic Arts, Eryl Porter, Dean Porter, Ellen Meltzer Porter, Joanna Pulcini, Harry and Kay Rabin, Suzanne Rosenblum, Fran Rubick, Lauren Deerfield St. Pierre, Daniel Scharlin, Noam Scheindlin, John and Lorene Scott, Kim Settle, Harriet Shaffer, Amy Smith, The Snite Museum of Art, Susan Solomon, Sarah Spencer, Mary Spivey, H.D. Spliid, David and Elizabeth Stroud, Karen Teitelbaum, Allan Temko, Ellen Thatcher, Sharon Thomas, Scott Underwood, University of California at Davis, University of Cincinnati School of Art, Architecture and Design, Richard Wahlberg, Dave Warden, Al and Peg Warren, Jane Warren, Joan Warren, Doug Wilcox, Burl Willis, Katrina Willis, Jon Winet, WNET/New York, Jeff and Anita Wray, Gina Costa Zachman, and Boris Zerafa.

In closing, we dedicate this book to Bill, Lorene, Morley, Roger, and Will—family and friends who passed away during the course of this project, whose support meant so much, and whose loss is deeply felt. They will always be remembered, as will the hundreds of unnamed Maya who so generously opened their homes, churches, cemeteries, and hearts to share stories of their lives and their colors. They all had much to teach us and even more to respect.

For information regarding limited-edition photographs of images in this book, please write to Jeffrey Becom, Post Office Box 534, Pacific Grove, California 93950-0534.

Waiting, Zunil, Guatemala

Candles, Santa María de Jesús, Guatemala

Sisters, Zunil, Guatemala

BIBLIOGRAPHY

Abrams, Elliot M. *How the Maya Built Their World: Energetics and Ancient Architecture.* Austin: University of Texas Press, 1994.

Acker, Alison. *Honduras: The Making of a Banana Republic.* Boston: South End, 1988.

Agurcia Fasquelle, Ricardo, and Juan Antonio Valdes. *Copan. Tikal. Secrets of Two Maya Cities.* San José: Credomatic, 1994.

Andrews, J. Richard, and Ross Hassig, trans. and eds. *Treatise on the Heathen Superstitions and Customs That Today Live Among the Indians Native to This New Spain, 1629,* by Hernando Ruiz de Alarcón. Norman: University of Oklahoma, 1984.

Annis, Sheldon. *God and Production in a Guatemalan Town.* Austin: University of Texas Press, 1987.

Arvigo, Rosita, with Nadine Epstein. *Sastun: My Apprenticeship with a Maya Healer.* San Francisco: HarperSanFrancisco, 1995.

"Attapulgite and Maya Blue: An Ancient Mine Comes to Light." *Archaeology* 1, no. 28 (1975): 23–29.

Attoe, Wayne O., and Sydney H. Brisker. *Architecture of Ricardo Legorreta.* Austin: University of Texas Press, 1990.

Baer, Philip, and William R. Merrifield. *Two Studies on the Lacandones of Mexico.* Norman: University of Oklahoma, 1971.

Barrera Vásquez, Alfredo, ed. *Diccionario Maya Cordemex.* Mérida: Ediciones Cordemex, 1980.

Benson, Elizabeth P., ed. *Death and the Afterlife in Pre-Columbian America.* Washington, D.C.: Dumbarton Oaks, 1975.

Benson, Elizabeth P., and Gillett Griffin, eds. *Maya Iconography.* Princeton: Princeton University Press, 1988.

Beyer, Hermann. "El color negro, azul, y rojo en el simbolismo de los antiguos Mexicanos." In "Mito y simbología del México antigua," edited by Carmen Cook de Leonard, *El México Antigua* 10 (1965): 474–87.

Blom, Frans. *The Conquest of Yucatan.* New York: Cooper Square, 1971.

Blom, Gertrude, photographer. *Bearing Witness.* Edited by Alex Harris, Margaret Sartor, and Barry Norris. Chapel Hill and London: University of North Carolina Press, 1984.

Boone, Elizabeth. *The Murals of Bonampak.* Princeton: Princeton University Press, 1986.

———. ed. *Painted Architecture and Polychrome Monumental Sculpture in Mesoamerica.* Washington, D.C.: Dumbarton Oaks, 1985.

Brenner, Anita. *Idols behind Altars.* Cheshire: Biblo & Tannen, 1929.

Bricker, Victoria Reifler. *The Indian Christ, the Indian King: The Historical Substrate of Maya Myth and Ritual.* Austin: University of Texas Press, 1981.

———. *Ritual Humor in Highland Chiapas.* Austin and London: University of Texas Press, 1973.

Burns, Allan F. *Maya in Exile: Guatemalans in Florida.* Philadelphia: Temple University Press, 1993.

———. "The Caste War in the 1970's: Present-Day Accounts from Village Quintana Roo." In *Anthropology and History in Yucatán,* ed. Grant D. Jones (Austin: University of Texas Press, 1977), pp. 259–73.

Canby, Peter. *The Heart of the Sky: Travels among the Maya.* New York: HarperCollins, 1992.

Cancian, F. *Economics and Prestige in a Mayan Community: The Religious Cargo System in Zinacantan.* Stanford: Stanford University Press, 1965.

———. *Change and Uncertainty in a Peasant Economy: The Maya Corn Farmers of Zinacantan.* Stanford: Stanford University Press, 1972.

Carmack, Robert M. *Harvest of Violence: The Maya Indians and the Guatemalan Crisis.* Norman: University of Oklahoma Press, 1992.

Carmichael, Elizabeth, and Chloë Sayer. *The Skeleton at the Feast: The Day of the Dead in Mexico.* Austin: University of Texas Press, 1991.

Casas, Fray Bartolomé de las. *Apologética historia de las Indias.* Madrid: Serrano y Ganz, 1909.

Chamberlain, R. S. *The Conquest and Colonization of Honduras, 1502 to 1550.* Washington, D.C.: Carnegie Institute, 1953.

Chapman, Anne. *Los Hijos del Cópal y la Candela, Tomo I & II.* Centre d'Etudes Mexicaines et Centraméricaines, Instituto de Investigaciones Antropológicas Series 64 and 86. Mexico City: Universidad Nacional Antónoma de México, 1985–86.

Ciudad Real, Fray Antonio de. *Fray Alonso Ponce in Yucatan, 1588.* Translated by Ernest Noyes. New Orleans: Tulane University, 1932.

Clendinnen, Inga. *Ambivalent Conquests: Maya and Spaniard in Yucatan, 1517–1570.* Cambridge: Cambridge University Press, 1987.

Coe, Michael D. *America's First Civilization.* New York: American Heritage, 1968.

———. *The Maya.* New York: Thames and Hudson, 1993.

———. *The Maya Scribe and His World.* New York: Grolier Club, 1973.

Coe, Michael D., and Elizabeth Benson. *Atlas of Ancient America.* New York and Oxford: Facts on File, 1986.

Coe, Sophie D. *America's First Cuisines.* Austin: University of Texas Press, 1994.

Colby, Benjamin N., and Lore M. Colby. *The Daykeeper: The Life and Discourse of an Ixil Diviner.* Cambridge: Harvard University Press, 1981.

Collier, Anne Fishburne. *Law and Social Change in Zinacantan.* Stanford, Calif.: Stanford University Press, 1973.

Collier, George Allen. "Color Categories in Zinacantan." Thesis, Harvard College, 1963.

Cortés Ruiz, Efraín, et al. *The Days of the Dead, a Mexican Tradition*. Mexico City: GV Editores, 1991.

Craine, Eugene R., and Reginald C. Reindorp. *The Codex Pérez and the Book of the Chilam Balam of Maní*. Norman: University of Oklahoma Press, 1979.

Desmond, Lawrence Gustave, and Phyllis Mauch Messenger. *A Dream of Maya: Augustus and Alice Le Plongeon in Nineteenth-Century Yucatan*. Albuquerque: University of New Mexico Press, 1988.

Díaz del Castillo, Bernal. *The Discovery and Conquest of Mexico, 1517–1521*. Translated by A. P. Maudslay. New York: Farrar, Straus and Cudahy, 1956.

Dow, James W. "Saints and Survival: The Function of Religion in Central American Indian Society." Ph.D. diss., Brandeis University, Waltham, 1973.

Duby, Gertrude. "Los Tzotziles y los Tzeltales de Chiapas." In *Chiapas Indigena* (Mexico City: Universidad Nacional Antónoma de México, 1961).

Eber, Christine. *Women and Alcohol in a Highland Maya Town: Water of Hope, Water of Sorrow*. Austin: University of Texas Press, 1995.

Edmonson, Munro S., trans. and annotator. *The Ancient Future of the Itza: The Book of Chilam Balam of Tizimin*. Austin: University of Texas Press, 1982.

———. *Heaven Born Merida and Its Destiny: The Book of Chilam Balam of Chumayel*. Austin: University of Texas Press, 1986.

Edwards, Emily. *Painted Walls of Mexico from Prehistoric Times until Today*. With photographs by Manuel Alvarez Bravo. Austin: University of Texas Press, 1966.

Esser, Janet Brody, ed. *Behind the Mask in Mexico*. Santa Fe: Museum of New Mexico Press, 1988.

Everton, Macduff. *The Modern Maya: A Culture in Transition*. Albuquerque: University of New Mexico Press, 1991.

Fash, William L. *Scribes, Warriors and Kings: The City of Copan and the Ancient Maya*. New York: Thames & Hudson, 1993.

Florescano, Enrique. *Memory, Myth, and Time in Mexico: From the Aztecs to Independence*. Translated by Albert G. Bork and Kathryn R. Bork. Austin: University of Texas Press, 1994.

Freidel, David A., and Linda Schele. "Symbol and Power: A History of the Lowland Maya Cosmogram." Paper presented at the Princeton Conference, The Beginnings of Maya Iconography, October 1982.

Freidel, David A., Linda Schele, and Joy Parker. *Maya Cosmos: Three Thousand Years on the Shaman's Path*. New York: W. Morrow, 1993.

Frundt, Henry J. *Refreshing Pauses: Coca-Cola and Human Rights in Guatemala*. Westport, Conn.: Praeger, 1987.

Gann, Thomas. *The Maya Indians of Southern Yucatan and Northern British Honduras*. Smithsonian Institution, Bureau of Ethnology Bulletin 64. Washington, D.C., 1918.

García Maroto, Gabriel. *Arquitectura popular de México*. Introduction by Enrique Yañez. Mexico City: Instituto Nacional de Bellas Artes, 1954.

Gettens, Rutherford J. "Identification of Pigments on Fragments of Mural from Bonampak, Chiapas." In *Bonampak, Chiapas, Mexico,* edited by Karl Rupert, J.E.S. Thompson, and Tatiana Proskouriakoff (Washington, D.C.: Carnegie Institution, 1955).

Glassman, Paul. *Guatemala Guide*. Champlain, Ill.: Passport Press, 1990.

Gossen, Gary H. *Chamulas in the World of the Sun: Time and Space in a Maya Oral Tradition*. Cambridge: Harvard University Press, 1974.

———, ed. *Symbol and Meaning Beyond the Closed Community: Essays in Mesoamerican Ideas*. Austin: University of Texas Press, 1986.

Guiteras-Holmes, C. *Perils of the Soul: The World View of a Tzotzil Indian*. Afterword by Sol Tax. New York: Free Press of Glencoe, 1961.

Hammond, Norman, ed. *Cuello: An Early Maya Community in Belize*. New York: Cambridge University Press, 1991.

Harbury, Jennifer. *Bridge of Courage: Life Stories of the Guatemalan Compañeros and Compañeras*. Monroe: Common Courage Press, 1994.

Huezo, Roberto, Gilberto Aguilar Aviles, and Federico Trujillo. *El Salvador: Un Rincón Mágico*. San Salvador: Banco Agricola Comercial de El Salvador, 1994.

Jones, Grant D. *Maya Resistance to Spanish Rule: Time and History on a Colonial Frontier*. Albuquerque: University of New Mexico Press, 1989.

Karasik, Carol, ed. *The People of the Bat: Mayan Tales and Dreams from Zinacantán*. Compiled and translated by Robert M. Laughlin. Washington D.C. and London: Smithsonian Institution Press, 1988.

Kelley, David H., and Heinrich Berlin. *The 819-Day Count and Color-Direction Symbolism among the Classic Maya*. New Orleans: Tulane University, 1961.

Kintz, Ellen R. *Life under the Tropical Canopy: Tradition and Change among the Yucatec Maya*. Fort Worth: Holt, Rinehard and Winston, 1990.

Landa, Friar Diego de. *Yucatan before and after the Conquest*. Translated and with notes by William Gates. New York: Dover, 1978.

Laughlin, Robert M. *The Great Tzotzil Dictionary of San Lorenzo Zinacantán*. Washington, D.C.: Smithsonian Institution Press, 1975.

———. *Of Shoes and Ships and Sealing Wax: Sundries from Zinacantán*. Contributions to Anthropology 25. Washington, D.C.: Smithsonian Institution Press, 1980.

———. *Of Wonders Wild and New: Dreams from Zinacantán.* Contributions to Anthropology 22. Washington, D.C.: Smithsonian Institution Press, 1976.

Leon-Portilla, Miguel. *Time and Reality in the Thought of the Maya.* Norman: University of Oklahoma Press, 1988.

———, ed. *The Broken Spears: The Aztec Account of the Conquest of Mexico.* Boston: Beacon Press, 1962.

López Morales, Francisco Javier. *Arquitectura vernácula en Mexico.* Mexico City: Editorial Trillas S.A. de C.V., 1993.

Loten, H. Stanley, and David M. Pendergast. *A Lexicon for Maya Architecture.* Toronto: Royal Ontario Museum, 1984.

Love, Bruce. *The Paris Codex: Handbook for a Maya Priest.* Introduction by George E. Stuart. Austin: University of Texas Press, 1994.

McGee, R. Jon. *Life, Ritual and Religion among the Lacandón Maya.* Belmont, Calif.: Wadsworth, 1990.

Manuel, Anne, and Eric Stover. *Guatemala: Getting Away with Murder.* New York: Americas Watch, 1991.

Markman, Roberta H., and Peter T. Markman. *The Flayed God: The Mythology of Mesoamerica.* San Francisco: Harper, 1993.

Markman, Sidney David. *Arquitectura y urbanización en el Chiapas colonial.* Chiapas, Mexico: Gobierno del Estado de Chiapas, DIF Chiapas, y Instituto Chiapaneco de Cultura, 1993.

Menchú, Rigoberta. *I, Rigoberta Menchú: An Indian Woman in Guatemala.* New York: Routledge, Chapman & Hall, 1985.

Miller, Mary Ellen. *The Murals of Bonampak.* New Jersey: Princeton University Press, 1986.

Miller, Mary Ellen, and Karl Taube. *The Gods and Symbols of Ancient Mexico and the Maya: An Illustrated Dictionary of Mesoamerican Religion.* London: Thames and Hudson, 1993.

Molina F., Diego. *Las confesiones de Maximón.* Guatemala City: Artemis y Edinter, 1983.

Montejo, Victor. *Testimony: Death of a Guatemalan Village.* Translated by Victor Perera. Willimantic, Conn.: Curbstone Press, 1987.

Moriarty, Steve. *Stories from Salvador: Photographs by Steve Moriarty.* Notre Dame, Ind.: Snite Museum of Art, 1991.

Morley, Sylvanus G. and George W. Brainerd. *The Ancient Maya.* Revised by Robert J. Sharer. Stanford, Calif.: Stanford University Press, 1983.

Morris, Walter F., Jr. *Living Maya.* Photographs by Jeffrey Jay Foxx. New York: Harry N. Abrams, 1987.

Muñoz, Luis Lujan, and Miguel Alvarez Arevalo. *Imágenes de Oro, Galeria Guatemala II.* Guatemala City: G & T Corporación, 1993.

Naggar, Carole, and Fred Ritchin, eds. *México Through Foreign Eyes / Visto por ojos extranjeros, Photographs 1850–1990.* New York and London: W. W. Norton, 1993.

Nájera Coronado, Martha Ilia. *Bonampak.* México City: Gobierno del Estado de Chiapas, Espejo de Obsidiana Ediciones, 1991.

Nash, June C. *In the Eyes of the Ancestors: Belief and Behavior in a Maya Community.* New Haven: Yale University Press, 1970.

Oakes, Maud. *The Two Crosses of Todos Santos: Survivals of Mayan Religious Ritual.* Introduction by Paul Radin. New York: Pantheon Books, 1951.

Ochiai, Kazuyasu. "When the Saints Come Marching In: Inter-Community Public Rituals among the Tzotzil Indians of Southeastern Mexico." Diss., University of New York at Albany, 1983.

Parker, Ann, with text by Avon Neal. *Los Ambulantes: The Itinerant Photographers of Guatemala.* Cambridge and London: Massachusetts Institute of Technology Press, 1982.

Parry, Robert. *Trick or Treason: The October Surprise Mystery.* New York: Sheridan Square Press, 1993.

Patch, Robert W. *Maya and Spaniard in Yucatan, 1648–1812.* Stanford, Calif.: Stanford University Press, 1993.

Paz, Marco de, and Marcus de Paz. *The Mayan Calendar: The Infinite Path of Time.* Guatemala City: Ediciones Gran Jaguar 2, 1993.

Pearce, Kenneth. *The View from the Top of the Temple.* Albuquerque: University of New Mexico Press, 1984.

Peissel, Michel. *The Lost World of Quintana Roo.* New York: E. P. Dutton, 1963.

Perera, Victor. *Rites: A Guatemalan Boyhood.* San Francisco: Mercury House, 1994.

———. *Unfinished Conquest: The Guatemalan Tragedy.* With photographs by Daniel Chauche. Berkeley: University of California Press, 1993.

Perera, Victor, and Robert D. Bruce. *The Last Lords of Palenque: The Lacandon Mayas of the Mexican Rain Forest.* Berkeley: University of California Press, 1985.

Perry, Richard. *Mexico's Fortress Monasteries.* Santa Barbara, Calif.: Espadaña Press, 1992.

———. *More Maya Missions: Exploring Colonial Chiapas.* Santa Barbara. Calif.: Espadaña Press, 1994.

Perry, Richard, and Rosalind Perry. *Maya Missions: Exploring the Spanish Colonial Churches of Yucatán.* Santa Barbara, Calif.: Espadaña Press, 1988.

Piña Chán, Román. *Jaina, la casa en el agua.* Mexico City: Instituto Nacional de Antropología e Historia, 1968.

Proskouriakoff, Tatiana. *Maya History.* Austin: University of Texas Press, 1993.

Redfield, Robert. *The Folk Culture of Yucatan.* Chicago: University of Chicago Press, 1941.

———. *A Village That Chose Progress: Chan Kom Revisited.* Chicago: University of Chicago Press, 1950.

Redfield, Robert, and Alfonso Villa Rojas. *Chan Kom: A Maya Village.* Chicago: University of Chicago Press, 1962.

Reed, Nelson. *The Caste War of Yucatán.* Stanford, Calif.: Stanford University Press, 1964.

Reyes-Valerio, Constantino. *De Bonampak al Templo Mayor: El Azul Maya en Mesoamérica.* Mexico City: Agro Asemex, Siglo Veintiuno Editores Sa. de Cv., 1993.

Robertson, Merle Green, ed. *The Palenque Round Table Series.* Volume 5. Austin: University of Texas Press, 1980.

Robicsek, Francis. *The Smoking Gods: Tobacco in Maya Art, History, and Religion.* Norman: University of Oklahoma Press, 1978.

Rosenbaum, Brenda. *"With Our Heads Bowed": The Dialectics of Gender in a Mayan Village.* Austin: University of Texas Press, 1992.

Ross, John. *Rebellion from the Roots: Uprising in Chiapas.* Monroe: Common Courage Press, 1995.

Roys, Ralph L., trans. and ed. *Ritual of the Bacabs.* Norman: University of Oklahoma Press, 1965.

Sahagún, Fray Bernadino de. *General History of the Things of New Spain.* Translated by Arthur J. O. Anderson and Charles E. Dibble. Santa Fe, N.M.: School of American Research, 1950–69.

Salas Portugal, Armando. *Barragán: photographs of the architecture of Luis Barragán.* New York: Rizzoli, 1992.

Saville, Marshall H., ed. "Reports on the Maya Indians of Yucatan." In *Indian Notes and Monographs,* vol. 9, no. 3, edited by F. W. Hodge. New York: Museum of the American Indian, Heye Foundation, 1921.

Sayer, Chloë. *The Mexican Day of the Dead: An Anthology.* Boston and London: Shambhala, 1994.

Schele, Linda, and David Freidel. *A Forest of Kings: The Untold Story of the Ancient Maya.* New York: William Morrow, 1990.

Schele, Linda, David Freidel, and Mary Ellen Miller. *The Blood of Kings: Dynasty and Ritual in Maya Art.* New York: George Braziller, 1992.

Schlesinger, Stephen, and Stephen Kinzer. *Bitter Fruit: The Untold Story of the American Coup in Guatemala.* New York: Doubleday, 1983.

Simon, Jean-Marie. *Guatemala: Eternal Spring, Eternal Tyranny.* New York: Norton, 1989.

Smith, Carol A., ed. *Guatemalan Indians and the State, 1540–1988.* Austin: University of Texas Press, 1990.

Stephens, John Lloyd. *Incidents of Travel in Central America, Chiapas, and Yucatan.* Vols. 1–2. New York: Dover, 1969.

Stierlin, Henri. *Living Architecture: Mayan.* New York: Grosset & Dunlap, 1964.

Stone, Andrea J. *Images from the Underworld: Naj Tunich and the Tradition of Maya Cave Painting.* Austin: University of Texas Press, 1995.

Stuart, Gene S., and George E. Stuart. *Lost Kingdoms of the Maya.* Washington, D.C.: National Geographic Society, 1993.

Tate, Carolyn E. *Yaxchilán: The Design of a Maya Ceremonial Center.* Austin: University of Texas Press, 1992.

Tedlock, Barbara. *Time and the Highland Maya.* Albuquerque: University of New Mexico Press, 1992.

Tedlock, Dennis. *Breath on the Mirror: Mythic Voices and Visions of the Living Maya.* San Francisco: HarperSanFrancisco, 1993.

———, trans. *Popol Vuh: The Mayan Book of the Dawn of Life.* New York: Simon & Schuster, 1985.

Thompson, J. Eric S. *Maya History and Religion.* Norman: University of Oklahoma Press, 1970.

———. "Sky Bearers, Colors and Directions in Maya and Mexican Religion." In *C.I.W. Pub. 436,* Contrib. 10, Washington, D.C., 1934.

Totten, George O. *Maya Architecture.* Washington, D.C.: Maya Press, 1926.

Ujpán, Ignacio Bizarro. *Ignacio: The Diary of a Maya Indian of Guatemala.* Edited by James D. Sexton. Vol. 3. Philadelphia: University of Pennsylvania Press, 1992.

Vogt, Evon Z. *Tortillas for the Gods: A Symbolic Analysis of Zinacanteco Rituals.* Cambridge and London: Harvard University Press, 1976.

———. *Zinacantan: A Maya Community in the Highlands of Chiapas.* Cambridge: Belknap Press, Harvard University, 1969.

Watanabe, John M. *Maya Saints and Souls in a Changing World.* Austin: University of Texas Press, 1992.

Wauchope, Robert. *Modern Maya Houses: A Study of Their Archaeological Significance.* Carnegie Institution of Washington, Publication 502. Washington, D.C., 1938.

Wilson, Carter. *Crazy February: Death and Life in the Mayan Highlands of Mexico.* Berkeley: University of California Press, 1974.

Wilson, Richard. *Maya Resurgence in Guatemala: Q'eqchi' Experiences.* Norman: University of Oklahoma Press, 1995.

Wright, Ronald. *Stolen Continents: The "New World" Through Indian Eyes.* Boston, New York, and London: Houghton Mifflin Company, 1992.

———. *Time among the Maya: Travels in Belize, Guatemala, and Mexico.* New York: Henry Holt and Company, 1989.

Yampolsky, Mariana. *Tlacotalpan: Village of Artists, Arte Hecho Pueblo.* Introduction by Elena Poniatowska. Mexico City: Instituto Veracruzano de la Cultura, 1987.

———. *The Traditional Architecture of Mexico.* Text by Chloë Sayer. London: Thames and Hudson, 1993.

INDEX